PURPOSE

A RENEWABLE ENERGY FUELING EDUCATORS

DR. RUSS QUAGLIA
&
DR. KRISTINE FOX

Copyright © 2025 by Dr. Russ Quaglia and Dr. Kristine Fox

All rights reserved.

No part of this publication may be reproduced, distributed, or transmitted in any form or by any means, including photocopying, recording, or other electronic or mechanical methods, without the prior written permission of the publisher, except in the case of brief quotations used in critical reviews and certain other noncommercial uses permitted by copyright law.

For permission requests, write to the publisher at:

Quaglia Institute

https://www.quagliainstitute.org/

First Edition

ISBN: 978-0-635-44640-4

Imprint: Quaglia Institute

With deepest gratitude and enduring respect, we dedicate this book to the students and educators who have inspired us, challenged us, and reminded us why this work is so important. Your courage to constantly strive for excellence despite adversity, and to lead with heart has fueled every page of this book. It is your values, passion, aspirations, and talents that gives our purpose meaning. We will forever believe in the extraordinary power that rises when students and educators join hands, dream boldly, and work together for each other, and for a better world.

Russ Quaglia & Kristine Fox

This book is a work of nonfiction. The stories, names, and examples used are based on real experiences and research in the field of education. Where necessary, identifying details have been changed to protect privacy.

For bulk orders, speaking engagements, or partnership inquiries, contact:

https://www.quagliainstitute.org/

Contents

INTRODUCTION   7
THE ROADMAP   11

Chapter 01
    Defining Purpose   13
Chapter 02
    Values: Our Guiding Light   33
Chapter 03
    Purpose Powered by Passion: 60
Chapter 04
    Vision and Voyage: 83
Chapter 05
    Purpose in Practice: 105
Chapter 06
    The Spark Within: 139
Chapter 07
    Shaping Tomorrow: 155

APPENDIX   176

INTRODUCTION

As I sit on the porch of my camp in Maine, surrounded by the stillness of the woods, I find myself reflecting on four decades of research, writing, and teaching. I've visited countless schools, met extraordinary educators and students, and had conversations that not only shaped my career but also the person I've become. The journey has been both humbling and transformative.

Throughout the years, I've witnessed the transformative power of *voice* and *aspiration* firsthand. I've heard hope in the questions of curious students, seen sparks of discovery ignite entire classrooms, and felt the energy that flows when teachers and students work together with *purpose*. In these moments, learning becomes more than a process—it transforms into a shared experience built on trust and respect, where ideas take shape, solutions emerge, and individuals take ownership—not just of their words, but of the actions that follow. Most importantly, I've seen both students and educators step into responsibility, not only for what is said, but for what needs to be done.

Yet alongside those moments of inspiration, I've also seen the weight of systemic challenges pressing down on education. Standardized testing has drained resources and stifled creativity, while bureaucratic constraints have chipped away at the autonomy of both teachers and students. Books have been censored, curiosity sidelined, and the vital link between learning and real-world application too often severed. In those moments, I felt disconnected, fatigued, and disillusioned. I began to question my *why*. Why had I chosen this career path? Why was I working so hard when it sometimes felt like it didn't matter? And the most honest question of all—why do I keep going despite all the challenges?

For me, the answer always came down to one word: *purpose*. My career was never about paychecks, test scores, or accolades. What fueled me was a deep-seated belief that education has the power to instill *self-worth*, foster *engagement*, and cultivate *purpose*. *Purpose* isn't an accessory—it is the very heart and soul of who I am as an educator.

Through reflection, I came to understand that *purpose* is the fuel that propels me toward both personal and professional goals. It inspires us to bring our best selves into the classroom, to meet challenges with a *can-do attitude*, and to nurture growth in our students. Educators who live with *purpose* are alive with energy, always learning, always adapting, and constantly rising to the demands of the profession.

I have felt the deep frustration of encountering educators who seemed more focused on themselves than their students, those who had lost sight of their *passion* and the deeper *why* behind their work. Yet every time I witnessed a student's eyes light up with understanding, or heard them excitedly share their dreams and ideas, my own *purpose* was reignited. Those moments serve as powerful reminders of why I chose this profession in the first place—and why so many dedicated educators continue to show up, give their best, and make a lasting impact, even in the face of mounting challenges.

It is these memories and experiences, both good and bad, that helped me reconnect with my *purpose* and gain clarity about who I am as an educator. And since I'm writing a book about *purpose*, I believe you should know mine. My life *purpose* is to help others recognize and realize their potential. I strive to ensure that every person I encounter feels a greater sense of *self-worth*, becomes more *meaningful*, and gains the *self-confidence* to make the world a better place for others. It's not an easy *purpose*, but it grounds me and gives me strength.

As educators, our greatest responsibility is not merely to impart knowledge but to unlock the potential within every student and colleague in our learning communities. This doesn't happen through fancy curricula, professional development workshops, complicated timetables, or even cutting-edge technology. It happens when we, as individuals, understand our *purpose*—when we know who we are, what we stand for, and how we can positively impact those around us. Educators with *purpose* possess *self-worth*, are deeply engaged in their work, and lead alongside their students and colleagues for the good of the whole.

Countless books have been written about discovering and living one's *purpose*—some are excellent, offering deep insights and real-world examples of success in action. Others fall short, presenting scattered thoughts and underdeveloped ideas. The well-crafted ones emphasize the significance of having a *purpose*, often illustrated through inspiring narratives. However, even the best of these works often miss something crucial: they fail to offer a framework that helps educators reflect on their *purpose* in a way that is both meaningful and sustainable. There is also a notable gap in defining the core elements that make up *purpose*. Without that clarity, many educators are left without the tools they need to identify, align with, and sustain their personal and professional motivations.

This book fills that gap. In the chapters ahead, we will explore the transformative power of *purpose* in education, *weaving together compelling stories, evidence-based research, and practical strategies*. The core elements of *purpose* will be clearly defined, and you'll be invited on a journey to discover your own unique motivations with clarity and precision.

We will also examine a frequently overlooked but critical dimension of professional life: the profound, far-reaching impact of our actions. As educators, it is essential that we pause from time to time to reflect on *why* we do what we do. This reflection not only rekindles our own commitment but also deepens our understanding of the ripple effects our teaching and interactions have on students, colleagues, their futures, and, by extension, the fabric of society itself.

In short, this book is here to reignite that spark of *passion* and remind us of the deeply rooted *reasons* behind our dedication to education.

It is my hope that this book inspires you to reflect on your journey, rediscover your *purpose*, and rekindle the *passion* that first drew you to this noble profession. I encourage you to think about what initially lit that fire within you, and what continues to sustain it today. Embracing your *purpose* will empower you to fully support your students, helping them find their *voices* and pursue their *dreams* with confidence.

As you read, approach each chapter with curiosity and an open heart. Give yourself the time and space to dive deeply into who you are, as both an educator and a person. Together, let's reignite the spark that inspired your calling, reaffirm the *values* that guide your work, and celebrate the vital role you play in shaping lives and building a better future.

THE ROADMAP

Before we delve deeper into *purpose* and introduce its four elements—*Values*, *Passions*, *Aspirations*, and *Talents*—we invite you to explore the visual roadmap below. As you progress through this book, your understanding of these elements' interconnectedness and their relationship to *purpose* will undoubtedly emerge.

The *"Elements of Purpose"* diagram illustrates the powerful and dynamic relationship among the four core components: *Values*, *Passion*, *Aspirations*, and *Talents*. The use of a *lemniscate* (infinity symbol) as the visual centerpiece emphasizes the continuous, cyclical nature of *purpose*. Each element flows organically into the next, affirming that living a *purposeful* life is not a straight line but rather a fluid journey of reflection, action, growth, and renewal.

The Flow of the Elements of Purpose

Purpose emerges from the powerful connection between four foundational elements: *Values, Passion, Aspirations,* and *Talents*. Each plays a distinct role, but it is their integration that creates a truly *meaningful, purpose-driven* life.

The journey often begins with *Values*—the core principles that shape our decisions and define what truly matters. When fully embraced, *values* act as an internal compass, guiding choices that are both authentic and aligned.

Passion is the emotional energy that fuels our engagement and commitment. When grounded in *values, passion* becomes a sustainable force, driving us toward meaningful pursuits rather than fleeting interests or superficial goals.

As *passion* deepens, it gives rise to *Aspirations*—future-oriented dreams and ambitions that reflect who we want to become and the impact we hope to make. When rooted in both *values* and *passion, aspirations* take on authenticity, representing goals that are personally meaningful rather than imposed by external pressures.

Talents bring *purpose* into action. These include innate abilities, learned skills, and lived experiences that allow individuals to translate *values-aligned aspirations* into reality. Through the development and application of their *talents*, people are able to contribute meaningfully, experience fulfillment, and achieve success.

These four elements are not isolated or linear; they are deeply interconnected in an ongoing, evolving cycle. *Values* ignite and inform *passion*. *Passion* energizes and shapes *aspirations*. *Aspirations* guide the cultivation and direction of *talents*. In turn, the practice and refinement of *talents* often lead back to deeper reflection on one's *values*, a renewed sense of *passion*, and the expansion of *aspirations*.

Each element strengthens and reinforces the others, creating a resilient and adaptable sense of *purpose*—one that evolves as we grow and respond to life's challenges and opportunities.

01 | Defining Purpose

The two most important days in your life are the day you are born and the day you find out why.

— **Mark Twain**

Once you become aware of the term *purpose*, you'll start noticing it everywhere—movies, commercials, political speeches, sitcoms, even viral internet posts. Consider the film *The Pursuit of Happyness*, where Chris Gardner's (Will Smith) relentless fight for a better life for his son beautifully embodies *purpose in action*. Commercials like Nike's *"Find Your Greatness"* urge individuals to push past limitations. Sitcoms explore the theme as well—*Friends*, for example, portrays Ross and Rachel as they navigate *purpose* through love, career, and personal growth. Political leaders routinely invoke *purpose* in speeches, using it to frame their vision for the future. From historical heroes like Martin Luther King Jr. and *Gandhi*, to contemporary figures and movements such as *Malala Yousafzai* and *Doctors Without Borders*, we see lives shaped and defined by a deep sense of *purpose*. Even modern internet culture is steeped in the idea, with influencers and self-help voices urging us to "live with *purpose*" as the secret to fulfillment.

Purpose is a word we hear often—people talk about *finding* their purpose, like college students exploring career paths; *realizing* it, like athletes dedicating themselves to excellence; *being driven* by it, like activists fighting for justice; and even *being saved* by it, as in stories of individuals overcoming addiction or personal crisis through a renewed sense of meaning. It's undeniably a powerful and popular concept—but do most people truly understand what it means?

Despite its frequent use, *purpose* is often misunderstood. It's commonly confused with a fleeting *passion* or a temporary *ambition*, rather than being recognized for what it truly is—a deeply rooted, enduring force that quietly but powerfully guides our choices, shapes our *values*, and gives direction to our lives.

Take a moment to reflect on your own *purpose*. It may sound like a simple task, but it's one of the most challenging and deeply personal questions you can ask yourself. Defining your *purpose* is hard for many reasons. It's rarely discussed openly. Few of us are taught how to think about it. And even fewer can clearly articulate what *purpose* truly means in their lives.

Words like *goal, plan, aspiration, vision,* and *objective* are often used as substitutes, but they don't quite capture the essence of *purpose*, especially for educators seeking to uncover or reignite their deeper *why*. To explore the real significance of *purpose*, we need a definition that is tangible and actionable—something that moves beyond abstract notions and brings us into a meaningful, grounded understanding.

The definition of purpose that this book will explore, understand, and hopefully encourage readers to reflect upon to make your own purpose clearer is the following:

Purpose is the driving force that gives meaning to educators' actions, reflecting their fundamental Values, Passions, Aspirations, and Talents. It serves as the energy that guides one's career, shapes decisions, motivates toward personal fulfillment, and contributes to the greater good.

Purpose is a **renewable source of energy, motivation, and direction** that powers one's life, endlessly replenished by personal *Values, Passions, Aspirations,* and *Talents*. Just as renewable energy harnesses natural forces for sustained power, a person's *purpose* draws from their intrinsic qualities and deepest desires to fuel continuous growth and meaningful achievement. This internal force empowers individuals to overcome obstacles, sparks innovation, and illuminates their path forward. When individuals align with their *purpose*, they not only contribute meaningfully to the world but also experience profound personal fulfillment.

Four key elements significantly shape an individual's sense of *purpose* and direction: *Values, Passion, Aspirations,* and *Talents.*

1. Values

Values are the moral standards and principles an individual holds most important. They guide decisions, influence behavior, and shape goals. When an educator's actions and career path are in alignment with their *values*, they experience greater integrity and fulfillment. Living in congruence with one's *values* is essential to cultivating a life of meaning and *purpose.*

2. Passion

Passions are intense feelings of enthusiasm and excitement for something meaningful. Often, they are the emotional fuel behind one's motivation and energy. *Passion* propels individuals to pursue activities, careers, or causes that bring deep joy and personal significance. When educators align their professional efforts with their *passions*, they are far more likely to experience a strong sense of satisfaction and *purpose* in their work.

3. Aspirations

Aspirations are one's hopes and dreams for the future, while also being inspired in the present to move toward those dreams. When educators are actively working toward their *aspirations*, they are fueled by a vision of what they wish to accomplish or become. The pursuit and realization of these *aspirations* can validate personal potential and deeply enhance an educator's sense of *purpose.*

4. Talents

Talents reflect the dynamic blend of a person's natural gifts, acquired skills, and lived experiences. This combination of innate strengths, learned abilities, and meaningful life interactions empowers individuals to live more *purpose-driven* lives. For educators, recognizing and embracing their *talents* fosters both personal growth and professional excellence and strengthens their ability to connect meaningfully with students, colleagues, and their broader community.

These four elements do not exist in isolation. They interact in a dynamic, ever-evolving cycle that continuously molds an educator's *purpose*. Each element feeds and enhances the others, shaping decisions, fueling motivation, and providing direction. When all four are in alignment, they energize educators to lead *purpose-driven* careers, characterized by both personal fulfillment and lasting impact.

Benefits of Purpose

Having a strong sense of *purpose* isn't just an abstract ideal—it's a powerful compass that guides individuals through life's complexities. A clear and compelling *purpose* infuses each day with renewed determination and enthusiasm, transforming routine actions into meaningful pursuits. It's not merely about setting goals; it's about aligning your actions with deeply held *values* that define who you are. This alignment not only helps you endure challenges—it also deepens your sense of fulfillment, making victories more meaningful and life more enriching.

Furthermore, a sense of *purpose* acts as a powerful buffer against life's inevitable stresses. It fosters *resilience*, allowing individuals to confront setbacks with confidence and transform obstacles into opportunities for growth. This *resilience* is rooted in the belief that every experience contributes to a larger narrative—one that you are actively shaping. With this perspective, adversity shifts from being a source of suffering to a catalyst for learning and self-improvement, strengthening your ability to adapt and thrive in an ever-changing world.

Purpose also extends well beyond professional fulfillment—it has a profound impact on overall *health* and *well-being*. Research shows that a strong sense of *purpose* acts as a protective factor against age-related decline in both physical and cognitive functioning (Lewis et al., 2017). As individuals move through adulthood, a well-defined *purpose* can foster greater *resilience*, enhance physiological health, and contribute to long-term cognitive vitality. Highlights from recent research include:

- **Longevity**: Individuals with *purpose* live longer and enjoy better cardiovascular health (Boyle et al., 2008).
- **Mental Health Improvement**: Strong *purpose* correlates with reduced depression and anxiety, offering a buffer for emotional well-being (Boreham & Schutte, 2023).
- **Reduced Risk of Alzheimer's Disease**: *Purpose* lowers the risk of Alzheimer's and supports mental *resilience* (Boyle et al., 2012).
- **Healthier Lifestyle Choices**: Purpose-driven individuals are more likely to exercise, avoid risky behaviors, and engage in preventative care (Kim et al., 2013).
- **Better Sleep**: A clear *purpose* improves sleep quality and reduces disturbances (Turner et al., 2017).

Beyond physical and mental benefits, a sense of purpose becomes even more vital in today's world, one marked by rapid technological change, political instability, environmental crises, and social upheaval. In such a dynamic and often unpredictable global climate, purpose fosters hope, instills confidence, and encourages proactive engagement. It becomes an inner anchor, enabling individuals to navigate uncertainty with courage and contribute meaningfully to society at large.

The Importance of Purpose in Contemporary Society

A sense of *purpose* can be understood as a stable and overarching intention to achieve something that is both *personally meaningful* and *impactful beyond the self*. In today's rapidly shifting global landscape, cultivating a strong sense of *purpose* is not just beneficial—it is essential for both individual and collective well-being. As mental health challenges continue to rise, fueled by global uncertainty, social unrest, and economic instability, a guiding *purpose* can serve as an emotional anchor, reducing susceptibility to depression and anxiety. While it doesn't erase life's problems, it offers a solid foundation to help navigate the chaos and irrationality of the modern world.

A strong sense of *purpose* is closely associated with several dimensions of well-being, including *optimism, positive affect, coping skills, personal growth, life satisfaction, emotional health, social connectedness, self-esteem*, and overall *psychological resilience*. It plays a particularly vital role in *emotional regulation*, especially in anxiety-inducing situations. Additionally, *purpose* functions as a powerful internal motivator, transforming routine tasks into meaningful actions and turning ordinary work into valuable contributions toward larger goals (Irving, 2024).

Consistent research findings show that individuals with a well-defined *purpose* experience significantly lower levels of stress and anxiety, along with higher levels of well-being. A strong sense of *purpose* is also linked to tangible health benefits: improved memory and cognitive function, better mood regulation, a lower risk of chronic disease and disability, and increased longevity (Godman, 2023). In this way, prioritizing *purpose* becomes not just a matter of motivation but a vital tool for enhancing both mental and physical resilience.

In today's evolving job market—where automation and artificial intelligence are redefining traditional roles—those who align their careers with broader life goals are more likely to adapt and thrive. Lin (2024) found that a strong sense of *meaning* in life significantly improves *career adaptability* among college students, underscoring the role of *purpose* in professional development and long-term success.

Aligning personal and professional goals not only increases job satisfaction but also fosters greater productivity, deeper learning, and ongoing adaptability. *Subjective well-being*—defined through *life satisfaction, happiness*, and *positive affect*—is strongly correlated with a sense of *purpose*. Those who are purpose-driven don't just feel more fulfilled in their careers—they are more capable of navigating daily challenges and setbacks, ultimately contributing to a healthier, more balanced life (Hill et al., 2018).

Importantly, *purpose* often extends beyond individual fulfillment. It includes a desire to contribute to something greater—to improve the lives of others, support communities, or build something of lasting value. *Purpose* is not just inward-looking; it is outward-reaching. It is about making a meaningful impact beyond oneself (Malin et al., 2017). It brings joy during good times and resilience during hard times—and this remains true across every season of life (Damon, 2008).

In an era marked by deep environmental challenges and persistent social inequities, cultivating a *communal sense of purpose* is essential. Purpose-driven initiatives have the power to transcend individual interests, promote collaboration and shared responsibility, and create lasting change. When personal *values* are aligned with collective needs, individuals and organizations alike can work together to build a more sustainable, equitable, and meaningful future.

The Amplified Importance for Educators

A strong sense of *purpose* is especially vital for educators. Whether you're a classroom teacher, educational assistant, school leader, counselor, coach, or serve in one of the many other essential roles within a school, your job is twofold: to navigate your own challenges within an ever-evolving educational landscape—and to carry the profound responsibility of instilling *purpose* in your students. By doing so, you empower the next generation to seek *meaning* in their own lives and careers.

Purpose-driven educators often emerge as leaders and innovators. Their *passion* and *expertise* not only elevate the learning experience, but they also inspire those around them, both colleagues and students alike. Their enthusiasm becomes contagious, creating a collaborative, positive work environment that increases engagement, strengthens productivity, and leads to greater success. Schools and systems that operate with a clear, shared *purpose* are more likely to attract and retain top talent, foster sustainable growth, and make lasting impacts. An educator's commitment to *purpose* is the very energy source that keeps them thriving in a profession known to drain one's batteries.

It's also important to remember: we are *role models* for our students, whether we realize it or not. How many of your teachers knew they were shaping your life? For us, the answer is virtually all of them—because we've made a conscious effort to tell them, even four decades later.

Students are always watching. Our attitudes, our *values*, and our behaviors are being observed—and often unconsciously adopted. An educator with a clear sense of *purpose* becomes a mirror for students to explore and refine their own. For example, a science teacher *passionate* about environmental sustainability may inspire students to pursue careers in conservation, engineering, or advocacy. A history teacher who emphasizes *critical thinking* and *ethical decision-making* can influence students to become socially conscious citizens—or even future policymakers.

An educator's influence often extends far beyond the lesson plan. Consider a coach who instills *perseverance* and *teamwork*, inspiring a student to build the leadership skills that define their future success. Or think of the school principal who nurtures *creativity* throughout the school, giving rise to a future writer, filmmaker, or journalist. These formative lessons stay with students long after graduation, guiding their values, decisions, and self-belief—often in ways they don't fully realize until much later in life.

Education today is in a constant state of reform. We are continually working to meet the demands of the 21st century and prepare students for a future that's still unfolding. Whether we are succeeding in this effort is a matter of perspective. But one truth stands out: educators who view their role through the lens of *purpose* are far more likely to embrace changes that enrich teaching and learning. Their commitment to student growth allows them to adapt more fluidly to new pedagogies, tools, and systems.

To be clear, having a strong sense of *purpose* doesn't make the life of an educator easier. But it does make the struggles, sacrifices, and adjustments more meaningful—and ultimately, more rewarding.

Educators with a strong sense of *purpose* are typically more engaged and persistent—qualities that have a direct, measurable impact on educational outcomes. Their *purpose-driven* approach often translates into higher expectations, deeper support, and more responsive teaching, creating environments where students feel safe to take risks, push boundaries, and excel both academically and personally. This mindset instills in learners the *courage* to embrace new experiences, pursue opportunities, and overcome the fear of failure (Quaglia, 2022).

Examining the *elements of purpose* through the lens of educators offers critical insight into what *purpose-driven education* truly looks like in practice. As you read through the following examples, reflect on your role in education and consider how these elements show up in your daily life.

Values

Educators exist in a constant whirlwind of shifting mandates, leadership transitions, and educational trends. Consider the conflicting approaches veteran teachers have witnessed over the years: *whole language vs. phonics, student-centered vs. teacher-centered learning, individualized vs. standardized instruction, academic rigor vs. social-emotional learning (SEL), zero-tolerance policies vs. restorative justice,* and debates over the *1619 Project* vs. *traditional American history*. The list goes on.

In the face of such uncertainty, one of the most effective ways for educators to maintain clarity and *purpose* is to identify and hold fast to their *core values*. These *values* become a stabilizing force, grounding not just teaching methods but also shaping one's overall *purpose* as an educator. When teachers are deeply rooted in their personal and professional *values*, they create learning environments that are both stable and authentic.

Moreover, educators who live by their *values* can model the same for students, encouraging them to reflect on and define their own. This reflection is essential for developing *responsible citizens* who are capable of navigating the moral and ethical complexities of modern society. Likewise, when school leaders act in alignment with strong *values*, their leadership becomes more transparent, trustworthy, and consistent— qualities that foster greater cohesion within school communities.

Passion

Think back to your very first year of teaching. The hours were long. The learning curve was steep. The paycheck was modest. And yet, despite the challenges, there was a fire inside you—a fierce commitment to make a difference. That fire was your *passion*.

Passion is what drives educators to stay up late crafting engaging lessons. It's what fuels extra time spent supporting struggling students. It's what brings joy when a child finally understands a difficult concept. Passionate educators do more than just deliver curriculum—they *inspire*. Their energy is contagious, sparking curiosity and igniting motivation in students. When a teacher is genuinely enthusiastic about a subject, students respond—they lean in, they ask questions, and they develop a love for learning.

But the impact of *passion* doesn't end at the classroom door. It radiates throughout entire school communities. It fosters collaboration among colleagues. It encourages continual professional development. It cultivates positive, resilient learning cultures. Without *passion*, educators may find themselves merely going through the motions—treating teaching as just another job instead of a *calling*.

Challenges in education are inevitable. But *passion* is what sustains educators through burnout, bureaucracy, and budget cuts. It's what makes teaching one of the most rewarding and transformative professions. When educators actively nurture and share their *passion*, they not only replenish their own motivation but also plant the seeds of *lifelong learning* in the hearts of their students.

Aspirations

Educators with clear *aspirations* have the unique ability to dream about the future while remaining deeply inspired in the present to bring those dreams to life (Quaglia, 2014). Having *aspirations* not only fuels personal motivation but also serves as a living example for students, showing them that *dreaming big* and *working diligently* are not just ideals but real possibilities.

When teachers *aspire* to something greater—whether it's advancing in their careers, refining their teaching methods, or making a lasting impact on students—they infuse their daily work with a heightened sense of *purpose*. Their aspirations are not about ambition for ambition's sake; they are grounded in a deeper *why* that fuels everything they do.

This same sense of *aspiration* applies across all roles in education. When school board members strive to create safe, inclusive environments or advocate for national education reform, they do so with a renewed *sense of purpose*. When mental health professionals within a school aspire to understand their communities better or reduce stigma surrounding emotional well-being, their goals bring clarity and *intentionality* to their role.

Aspirations help answer the foundational question: *Why?*
- Why do I dedicate so much time, energy, and heart to this profession?
- Why do I continue moving forward, even when the challenges feel overwhelming?

Educators with a clear vision of their *aspirations* answer these questions not with hesitation, but with conviction. For some, the goal may be to spark a lifelong love of learning. For others, it may be to help students build resilience, develop essential life skills, or pursue dreams that were never available to their own families. Imagine a middle school math teacher who *aspires* to change how students view mathematics, from something intimidating to something intriguing, a daily puzzle worth solving. Or consider a sixth-grade English teacher whose dream is to help students discover their voice through writing, equipping them to speak their truth with clarity and confidence.

Without *aspirations*, it becomes difficult—if not impossible—to develop a clear and enduring *sense of purpose*. Educators who drift without direction may begin to feel uninspired or stagnant. But those who consistently set, revisit, and pursue meaningful *aspirations* enrich their own professional journey—and serve as powerful catalysts for student transformation.

By *embracing aspirations*, educators create a ripple effect. They motivate and uplift, guiding students not just academically but emotionally and socially. In doing so, they help shape futures that extend far beyond the classroom walls, inspiring a new generation to aim higher, dream bigger, and believe in the power of their own potential.

Talents

Effective educators not only possess a strong set of teaching skills but are also committed to continually developing their professional abilities and adapting to new educational tools and methods. Many believe that "teachers are born into the profession," implying that some individuals naturally possess the gift of teaching, compassion, and communication. While there may be an element of innate talent, great educators are also shaped by their life experiences and professional development. When you take gifted strengths, coupled with life experiences, and infused with skill development, you have all the ingredients for a talented educator. It is important to note that the three above ingredients are not at the same levels for everyone. Each educator brings a unique combination of innate abilities, life experiences, and professional training to the classroom. For example, a teacher who has traveled extensively may bring a global perspective to geography class, enriching students' understanding of different cultures. Another educator who has worked in the corporate world before becoming a superintendent may offer valuable, unique perspectives on perennial school challenges. Similarly, an educational assistant with a background in theater might use set design ideas and performance to connect with her students. What we do know for sure is that talents equip educators to adapt to an ever-changing world and thus are inevitably life-long learners.

Ultimately, educators with a strong sense of purpose bring more than just knowledge to their students; they bring passion, direction, and a sense of meaning that can transform the learning experience. Teachers who are driven by purpose not only impart academic content but also inspire students to discover their own strengths and aspirations, creating a ripple effect that extends beyond the classroom and into the world.

Reflection

- What is your core purpose as an educator, and how does it align with your personal values?
- In what ways does your purpose influence your daily decisions and interactions with students, colleagues, and the school community?
- How do you actively communicate and demonstrate your purpose to colleagues, students, family, and friends?
- How has your professional purpose evolved throughout your career, and what experiences have contributed to these changes?

Impacts of Purpose in the Classroom

The *elements that comprise purpose* influence far more than just the lives of educators—they are equally critical to the development and well-being of students. A student's *self-worth, level of engagement*, and *ability to express their voice* all improve when they possess a sense of *purpose*.

In fact, students with a clear *sense of purpose* are 23% more likely to report a strong sense of *self-worth* (Quaglia, 2024). In this context, *self-worth* refers to students' perception of their own value and competence—an essential foundation for mental health and personal resilience. A well-defined *purpose* helps students recognize their unique contributions and affirm their place in the world. This affirmation, in turn, enhances self-esteem, boosts confidence, and encourages more positive peer and adult relationships. It becomes especially crucial in educational settings where students are constantly navigating academic pressure, social dynamics, and identity development. Feeling *valuable and capable* empowers them to manage these challenges more effectively, reducing both academic burnout and social alienation.

Research also shows that students with a defined *sense of purpose* are 44% more likely to be *meaningfully engaged* in their learning than their peers who lack it (Quaglia, 2024). Here, *engagement* goes beyond compliance or mere presence in class—it means being emotionally, intellectually, and even spiritually connected to learning. Purpose provides students with a compelling *why*, helping them see how their studies align with their long-term goals and dreams. When students perceive relevance in their education, they naturally lean in, participate more fully, and retain information more deeply. Their engagement shifts from passive consumption to active investment in their own growth.

What makes *purpose-driven motivation* so powerful is its *intrinsic nature*. Unlike motivation tied to grades, praise, or competition, purpose stems from within, anchored to personal meaning and long-term aspirations. This kind of motivation is more sustainable. It creates a positive feedback loop: *achievement reinforces purpose*, and *purpose fuels continued effort*. Students begin to view school not as a series of tasks, but as a platform for building the future they envision for themselves. This mindset shift doesn't just support academic achievement; it lays the foundation for *lifelong learning*.

Another powerful finding is that students with a strong sense of *purpose* are 43% more likely to report having a *voice* in school (Quaglia, 2024). This means they feel heard, respected, and empowered to express their ideas and beliefs. *Having a voice* is more than participation—it involves being part of meaningful dialogue, shaping decisions, and knowing that one's input matters. When students believe their voice has value, they begin to develop *core values*, *leadership skills*, and *collaborative abilities* that extend well beyond the classroom.

Purposeful students tend to be more engaged, more motivated, and more likely to take initiative. They seek leadership roles, advocate for change, and contribute positively to school culture. Their involvement often leads to improvements in classroom practices, school policies, and peer dynamics, enhancing the learning environment for everyone.

These findings highlight the *transformative power of purpose* in shaping students' educational experiences. When students feel purposeful, they develop greater *self-worth*, sustained *engagement*, authentic *motivation*, and a stronger *voice*. These outcomes not only foster academic success but also build the character, confidence, and resilience needed for life beyond school.

As educators, it is our *privilege and responsibility* to nurture these qualities. Helping students find and cultivate their *purpose* should be central to our mission. By modeling and integrating the four elements—*values*, *passion*, *aspirations*, and *talents*—into our own lives and teaching practices, we don't just educate minds; we shape futures. We prepare young people not just to succeed, but to live with meaning, contribute with heart, and lead with integrity.

Discussion

- What role should values play in your school? Classroom?
- How can educators use their passions as an energizer?
- How can administrators support teachers' aspirations?
- What natural talents do you admire in your colleagues? Why?

Purpose often arrives in the most unexpected places, and the key to embracing it is staying open, especially when the opportunity feels larger than life. Consider the timeless legend of *King Arthur*. As a young, unassuming boy, Arthur had no idea he was destined to lead a kingdom. Yet when he pulled the sword *Excalibur* from the stone—an act that only the true king could perform—his *purpose* was revealed. He didn't set out to rule, but he stepped forward when called. His journey wasn't just about power; it was about *courage, wisdom,* and *justice*. Arthur's story reminds us that *purpose* may not show up with a roadmap. It often unfolds through *obstacles, challenges,* and *unexpected turns,* and may require us to grow into roles we never imagined for ourselves.

The key takeaway from this chapter is simple but profound: ***purpose matters***. And *your purpose* matters.

When individuals connect with their unique sense of *purpose*, they tap into a force greater than motivation—it's *momentum with meaning*. This internal force not only drives personal growth and resilience but also elevates everyone around them. Whether you're leading a classroom, mentoring a colleague, or simply showing up for yourself, your *purpose* sends ripples of encouragement, strength, and change into the world.

In a culture that often values productivity over authenticity and hustle over *heart*, remembering and nurturing your *purpose* isn't a luxury—it's a necessity. It's what transforms the mundane into the meaningful, the ordinary into the extraordinary. It turns daily routines into acts of contribution and challenges into opportunities for growth.

Get Started: Renew Your Energy with Purposeful Actions

Here are a few ways to begin living—and leading—with renewed *purpose*:

- **Stay Open**

    Purpose evolves. What drives you today may shift tomorrow—and that's not only natural, it's essential. Stay curious and allow your purpose to grow with you.

- **Embrace Uncertainty**

    Finding your *purpose* isn't a straight path. It will include detours, disappointments, and doubt. Be willing to *explore, fail,* and *try again*. Every experience holds a clue.

- **Surround Yourself with Like-Minded People**

    Energy is contagious. Being around others who are passionate and purposeful can spark clarity and courage within you. Let their fire light yours.

- **Take Small Steps**

    You don't need to have it all figured out. Start where you are. One conversation, one choice, one step at a time. The journey builds from there.

- **Trust Your Instincts**

    You already hold a quiet knowing. If something *resonates*, even if it's unconventional, lean in. *Purpose* is less about logic and more about *truth*.

- **Create Quiet Time**

  In a noisy world, your inner voice often whispers. Make time for reflection—whether it's journaling, meditating, or walking in silence. When the mind is still, clarity finds its way in.

Purpose isn't just something you find. It's something you grow into—day by day, choice by choice. Embrace it, nurture it, and let it illuminate the path ahead. Your life, your work, and your world will be richer because of it.

Reflections from the Field

When a school runs on purpose, not just policy, it creates a sense of direction. Everyone understands what we're working toward—and why it matters. High School Principal

Teaching with purpose means I'm not just covering content; I'm helping students uncover who they are and who they can be. Middle School Social Studies Teacher

When students understand that PE isn't just about games but about building lifelong habits, they see a purpose in movement, and that changes how they show up. Physical Education Teacher and Coach

A school grounded in purpose doesn't just educate minds—it nurtures values, vision, and a future every student can believe in. Middle School Assistant Principal

Purpose means having a reason to work hard, even when it's boring or tough. It's what helps me keep going. 7th Grade Student

When young learners feel their efforts matter, purpose fuels their curiosity and turns small victories into lasting confidence. Elementary Language Arts Teacher

Purpose gives teenagers a reason to push through the hard days—it helps them see the 'why' behind the 'what' we teach. High School Math Teacher

Purpose is like a goal that actually means something to you. It's what helps you decide what kind of person you want to be. 10th Grade Student

Helping students find a sense of purpose gives them direction and reminds them that their life can go somewhere, even if it's tough right now. School Social Worker

Sometimes it's the little things—like showing up or finishing an assignment—that help students feel like they're moving forward with a purpose. Elementary Educational Assistant

When students understand the purpose behind caring for their minds and bodies, they begin to make choices that shape not just their health, but their future. 9th Grade Health Teacher

When my child sees that school has a purpose beyond just grades, they start showing up with more pride and more motivation. Parent

Purpose is the reason why we learn stuff. Like how reading helps me write stories, or helps my little brother. 3rd grade student

References

Boreham, P., & Schutte, N. S. (2023). Purpose in life and mental health: A meta-analytic review. *Journal of Positive Psychology, 18*(2), 243-258.

Boyle, P. A., Buchman, A. S., Barnes, L. L., & Bennett, D. A. (2012). Effect of purpose in life on the relation between Alzheimer's disease pathologic changes and cognitive function in advanced age. *Archives of General Psychiatry, 69*(5), 499-505.

Boyle, P. A., Barnes, L. L., Buchman, A. S., & Bennett, D. A. (2008). Purpose in life is associated with mortality among community-dwelling older persons. *Psychosomatic Medicine, 70*(5), 443-447.

Damon, W. (2008). *The path to purpose: Helping our children find their calling in life*. Free Press.

Godman, H. (2023, November 1). *10 ways to find purpose in life*. Harvard Health.

Hill, P. L., Sin, N. L., Turiano, N. A., Burrow, A. L., & Almeida, D. M. (2018). Sense of purpose moderates the associations between daily stressors and daily well-being. *Annals of Behavioral Medicine, 52*(8), 724-729.

Irving, J. (2024). "Just get up and get on." Purpose in later life. *Activities, Adaptation & Aging, 49*(1), 1–23.

Kim, E. S., Sun, J. K., Park, N., Kubzansky, L. D., & Peterson, C. (2013). Purpose in life and reduced incidence of stroke in older adults: The Health and Retirement Study. *Journal of Psychosomatic Research, 74*(5), 427-432.

Lewis, N. A., Turiano, N. A., Payne, B. R., & Hill, P. L. (2017). Purpose in life and cognitive functioning in adulthood. *Aging, Neuropsychology, and Cognition, 24*(6), 662-671.

Lin, X. (2024). Purpose in life and career adaptability: Examining meaning in life among college students. *Frontiers in Psychology, 15*.

Malin, H., Liauw, I., & Damon, W. (2017). Purpose and character development in early adolescence. *Journal of Youth and Adolescence, 46*, 1200–1215.

Turner, A. D., Hall, M. H., & Kim, E. S. (2017). A purpose in life and reduced incidence of sleep disturbances. *Psychosomatic Medicine, 79*(2), 126-131.

Quaglia, R., & Corso, M. (2014). Student Voice: The Instrument of Change. Corwin. Thousand Oaks, CA.

02 | Values: Our Guiding Light

I have learned that as long as I hold fast to my beliefs and values - and follow my own moral compass - then the only expectations I need to live up to are my own.

- Michelle Obama

> Values are the moral standards and principles that an individual holds important in their life. Values guide decisions, influence behavior, and shape goals. When an educator's actions and career path align with their values, they achieve a greater sense of integrity and fulfillment. Living in congruence with one's values is crucial for feeling that one's life has meaning and purpose.

Finding genuine purpose requires more than ambition or a five-year plan—it demands a deep, unwavering understanding of your *values*. These are the invisible threads that tie your identity, decisions, and interactions into a coherent whole. You might not always name them aloud, but your *values* are always present. They guide your path, influence your choices, and quietly shape your sense of right and wrong. Much like a compass points north, *values* give purpose its *true direction*. Without them, even the most driven ambition risks veering off course.

Why are *values* so essential? Because they define what truly matters to you. They're not just preferences—they are personal truths. They help answer life's bigger questions: *What kind of person do I want to be? What kind of impact do I hope to leave?* A person who holds *compassion* and *kindness* as core values might find deep satisfaction in helping professions—teaching, counseling, medicine, or social work. Someone who treasures *creativity* and *innovation* might be drawn toward design, entrepreneurship, or the arts. When your *daily choices* and *long-term goals* align with your values, your life feels not only meaningful but also congruent and whole.

Here's the truth: You cannot chase *purpose* without knowing your *values*. Trying to do so is like trying to play darts blindfolded. You might hit something, but it probably won't be the target. And it might hurt. *Values* are the bedrock upon which *purpose* stands. Without that foundation, purpose becomes vague, unsteady, and easily disrupted.

Values also serve as a renewable fuel source for motivation and resilience. Life, after all, isn't one big highlight reel. Students face academic stress, sleepless nights, social pressure, and identity confusion. There are moments when nothing makes sense, and even coffee can't fix it. But when students hold determination as a value, they persist. They'll shift their study strategy instead of giving up. And when is integrity a guiding principle? That's the voice that whispers, "Don't cheat," even when failure seems imminent and everyone else is cutting corners.

Equally important, values foster authenticity, which is at the core of personal fulfillment. To be authentic means your thoughts, feelings, and actions align (Harter, 2002). When your behavior reflects your beliefs, you feel grounded, more confident, more clear, more at peace. In contrast, living out of sync with your values creates inner tension. Imagine someone who values family and balance, but takes a job that demands nonstop travel, late hours, and constant availability. That misalignment may bring prestige or income, but it will never feel right. Recognizing that conflict is the first step toward realignment—toward living a life that mirrors what matters most.

In the end, *values* are more than ideals. They are anchors in chaos, guardrails on sharp turns, and the quiet voice that says, *"This is who I am."* When you honor them, you don't just find your *purpose*—you live it.

Beyond *personal fulfillment*, *values* shape how we show up in the world. They are the compass not just for our inner life, but for our relationships, careers, and communities. Values like *justice*, *equality*, and *community* don't just shape our choices—they ignite movements. They compel ordinary people to take extraordinary action, to stand in the face of injustice, and to build something better not only for themselves, but for others. For many, *purpose* becomes less about success and more about *significance*.

Consider the lives of individuals like *The Rev. William J. Barber II, Angela Doyinsola Aina, Greg Asbed, Lucas Benitez,* and *Laura Germino*. Each one embodies the power of leading with *values*. These are not celebrities or icons from centuries past. They are contemporary changemakers—living, breathing examples of how deep convictions can fuel a life of

Article

purposeful action. Their stories remind us that purpose isn't found—it's forged in the fires of what we stand for.

Why are *values* so essential in finding genuine *purpose*? Because they ground life's pursuits in something deeper than ambition or applause. They offer:

- *Guidance* when decisions feel unclear.
- *Motivation* when challenges seem overwhelming.
- *Authenticity* when life pressures us to conform.
- *Contribution* when we seek to make a difference in the world.

When *your values* and *your actions* are aligned, you feel anchored. Life doesn't just move forward—it moves forward in the *right direction*. And that is the key to living a life of *fulfillment, purpose,* and *lasting impact*.

Consider This: A List of Commonly Accepted Core Values

Take a moment to reflect on which of these values deeply resonate with you:

- **Adaptability** – Being able to adjust to new conditions.
- **Compassion** – Showing kindness and understanding toward others.
- **Courage** – Standing up for one's beliefs despite fear.
- **Creativity** – Valuing original thought and expression.
- **Empathy** – Understanding and sharing the feelings of others.
- **Equality** – Believing in equal rights and opportunities for all.
- **Fairness** – Treating others in a just and equitable manner.
- **Freedom** – Valuing independence and autonomy.
- **Generosity** – Giving freely to others without expecting anything in return.
- **Gratitude** – Being thankful for what one has.
- **Honesty** – Being truthful and sincere.
- **Humility** – Having a modest opinion of one's own importance.
- **Integrity** – Acting according to one's beliefs and principles.
- **Justice** – Upholding fairness and moral rightness.
- **Love** – Caring deeply for others.
- **Loyalty** – Remaining faithful and devoted to someone or something.
- **Optimism** – Looking at the brighter side of situations.
- **Patience** – Waiting calmly for something without frustration.
- **Perseverance** – Persisting in an endeavor despite difficulties.
- **Respect** – Showing consideration and regard for others.
- **Responsibility** – Being accountable for one's actions.
- **Security** – Valuing safety and stability in life.
- **Self-Respect** – Maintaining dignity and self-esteem.
- **Trust** – Being reliable and trustworthy in relationships.
- **Wisdom** – Having a deep understanding and insight.

Ultimately, *purpose* is not a treasure we stumble upon by accident. It's something we cultivate—day by day, choice by choice—through a deeper understanding of ***who we are*** and ***what matters most***. When we lead

Activity
Appendix A

with *values*, our *purpose* becomes not only *clearer* but also more *powerful*, more *authentic*, and infinitely more *sustainable*.

Reflection
1. Which three values resonate the most with you?
2. How do these values show up in your daily actions and decisions?
3. Are there any values you'd like to prioritize more in your life or work?
4. How do your values influence your goals or sense of purpose?
5. Can you think of a time when one of these values helped you overcome a challenge?

The Importance of Values for Educators

Values in education extend far beyond the walls of individual classrooms—they are foundational to the very architecture of global learning systems. Across the world, the *transmission of human values* plays a central role in how nations design, implement, and assess education (Matthes, 2014; Beck, 1990; Halstead, 1996). Many national curricula are intentionally grounded in values that are considered essential for the health and progression of society.

Consider a few compelling examples:
- England's National Curriculum and Ofsted standards highlight *core values* like democracy, mutual respect, and individual liberty as essential pillars of learning.
- Switzerland's Lehrplan 21 weaves *values* directly into its educational framework, creating a balance between cognitive skills and character development.
- Finland's curriculum gives equal weight to academic content and human values, treating both as co-drivers of education.
- Hong Kong's Education Bureau places strong emphasis on *values education*, nurturing qualities such as respect, responsibility, perseverance, and national identity.

What these systems reveal is simple and profound: education is never value-neutral. Every classroom, policy, and curriculum carries a vision—not just of what students should know, but of who they should become.

Educators themselves are no exception. Their daily choices—how they teach, respond, discipline, or uplift—are driven by their *personal values* (and, yes, probably caffeine). A teacher who prioritizes *compassion* and *responsibility* will go the extra mile for a struggling student, adapting their teaching to ensure every child feels seen and supported. A school leader who values *opportunity* may tirelessly advocate for equitable access to resources, fostering an inclusive culture where every student is empowered to thrive.

It's important to emphasize: it is not an educator's role to determine a student's values. Educators have influence, but not authority over a student's inner world. Their job is not to dictate what students should believe, but to *guide them* in discovering and defining what they already feel, think, and stand for.

This happens through modeling. Teachers who embody *integrity*, *curiosity*, *respect*, or *resilience* create cultures where these values are not lectured, but lived. It also happens through inquiry. A classroom rich in reflection and dialogue encourages students to ask the hard, meaningful questions: *What matters to me? Why do I care about this? How do my values show up in my choices?*

For example, in a government class examining civil rights movements, a teacher might disclose their commitment to *justice*, then open the floor to student dialogue, not to echo their view, but to explore diverse perspectives. During a debate or literature circle, teachers can help students reflect on ethical dilemmas and connect their reasoning back to personal beliefs.

It's also essential to recognize that *value systems differ*—sometimes subtly, sometimes dramatically. A teacher who prizes *punctuality* might encounter a student who values *creativity* and thrives in less rigid environments. A student raised in a *collectivist* culture may prioritize *community*, while their teacher emphasizes *individual responsibility*. A counselor who believes in *restorative justice* may work with a family advocating for more punitive consequences.

These differences are not *problems*—they are opportunities. Opportunities for mutual understanding, critical thinking, and the development of empathetic, culturally-aware citizens. In embracing these conversations, educators don't just pass on knowledge—they cultivate the wisdom, compassion, and complexity our world so desperately needs.

Importantly, educators must avoid assuming that students will—or should—adopt the same values they hold. When teachers impose their own beliefs, however well-intentioned, they risk silencing student voices and stifling independent thought. This can lead to classrooms that reflect conformity rather than curiosity. Instead, educators should act as facilitators of growth, encouraging students to reflect on their evolving identities while providing safe, inclusive spaces to explore ideas, question assumptions, and even challenge societal norms.

The goal of education is not to mold replicas of the adults in the room—it is to empower students to define and live by their own values. When students feel seen, heard, and supported in this process, they not only thrive academically but also grow into individuals equipped with confidence, self-awareness, and a deeply rooted sense of purpose.

That said, educators themselves must possess a clearly defined set of values. A teacher who values lifelong learning might continuously pursue new instructional strategies, adapting even in the face of setbacks. A school leader who values community might build a culture of open communication and collaborative leadership, strengthening trust among staff, students, and families. A counselor who values organization and strategic thinking might guide students through academic planning, helping them set goals and design roadmaps for college, career, or life readiness.

Video

When educators lack clarity in their values, challenges arise. Decision-making becomes inconsistent, relationships feel transactional, and professional fulfillment may erode. In contrast, values offer a steady compass, especially during periods of uncertainty.

One of the most vivid examples of this was the COVID-19 pandemic, which posed an unprecedented challenge to educators across the globe. Amid lockdowns, shifting expectations, and a rapidly digitizing world, the most effective teachers didn't just survive—they led with purpose, anchored by their values. Consider the following examples:

- **Adaptability:** Teachers embraced technology, quickly integrating platforms like Zoom, Google Classroom, and interactive apps to deliver lessons. Some got creative, turning to TikTok or YouTube to make learning engaging and accessible for students from all walks of life.
- **Compassion:** Recognizing the emotional toll of the crisis, educators prioritized connection over content. Many checked in on students' mental health through virtual calls, personalized messages, and outreach to families, showing that care isn't bound by classroom walls.
- **Equity:** Teachers who valued inclusivity worked tirelessly to bridge digital divides—delivering printed materials to students without internet, recording lessons for those with limited schedules, and advocating for equitable access to resources.
- **Resilience:** Educators who embodied perseverance used the crisis as a catalyst to reimagine learning. They didn't wait for a return to "normal"—they built new ways forward, rooted in creativity, empathy, and human connection.

These examples prove that in times of crisis, it's not curriculum guides or test scores that sustain educators—it's values. And when values are clear, they lead to purposeful action.

Active Learning: Rather than relying solely on traditional lectures, teachers created dynamic virtual experiences using gamified platforms like *Kahoot* and *Quizizz*, facilitated breakout room discussions, and assigned hands-on projects students could complete at home.

Fairness: Acknowledging the wide disparities in students' home environments, teachers implemented flexible deadlines, recorded lessons for asynchronous access, and offered differentiated assignments tailored to meet diverse learning needs.

Responsibility: Educators promoted student autonomy by designing choice-based assignments, self-paced modules, and independent research projects that empowered students to take ownership of their learning journey.

Perseverance: Despite the challenges of remote learning, teachers worked diligently to foster classroom communities through virtual check-ins, online clubs, themed dress-up days, and interactive activities like virtual field trips.

Empathy: Understanding the emotional weight of the pandemic, teachers incorporated mindfulness practices, created space for open mental health conversations, and implemented flexible classroom policies to reduce student stress.

Creativity: Assessment practices evolved as educators moved beyond traditional exams, exploring innovative alternatives like video presentations, digital portfolios, peer assessments, and project-based learning to engage students meaningfully.

Gratitude: With grace and patience, educators acknowledged the challenges faced by students, families, and colleagues alike, cultivating a culture of kindness, encouragement, and mutual support.

Optimism: Teachers maintained a forward-looking mindset, helping students remain motivated and resilient by focusing on hope and the promise of brighter days ahead.

Values are not just abstract ideals; they are the foundation of an educator's professional and personal life. They shape decisions, guide relationships, inform ethics, drive personal and professional growth, and provide emotional grounding in times of uncertainty. Without clearly defined values, educators are more likely to face burnout, dissatisfaction, and disconnection from their work. However, by clarifying and embracing their core values, educators cultivate careers rooted in purpose—careers that uplift not only themselves but also the students and communities they serve.

Recognizing the central importance of values is the first essential step toward building a life—and a legacy—of meaningful, purpose-driven education.

Challenges with Lack of Clarity in Values

1. Lack of Direction and Purpose

Educators without clearly defined values may feel aimless, unsure of what they want from their careers or personal lives. Values help prioritize aspirations and clarify what truly matters. Without them, decisions become reactive rather than intentional, and long-term goals lose meaning. For example, a teacher who values innovation might actively seek out professional development opportunities to refine their instructional methods. In contrast, an educator without a guiding value system may drift from job to job, unsure of where they belong or what brings them genuine fulfillment.

2. Decision-Making Paralysis

Values serve as a trusted framework for decision-making, offering clarity in moments of uncertainty. Without them, choices become more difficult, often leading to indecision, second-guessing, and regret. Consider an educator weighing whether to accept a leadership role or remain in the classroom. If they value mentorship, they might find purpose in guiding others through leadership. If they prioritize direct student impact, they may choose to stay close to teaching. But without defined values, either path can feel confusing and unsatisfying.

3. Increased Susceptibility to External Pressures

In the absence of strong personal values, educators can become vulnerable to outside influence, whether from peer expectations, institutional demands, or societal trends. This often leads to disconnection from one's authentic voice. For instance, a teacher who values student-centered learning may feel pressured to conform to a rigid, test-driven curriculum. Without the confidence to advocate for their beliefs, they may compromise their teaching philosophy, leading to frustration, internal conflict, and burnout.

4. Weakened Relationships

Values influence how educators interact with students, colleagues, and families. When these guiding principles are unclear or inconsistent, relationships may become strained or superficial. A teacher who values inclusivity, for instance, will intentionally build a classroom where every student feels seen and valued. Without that clarity, relational efforts may feel disjointed, resulting in miscommunication, missed connections, and lower student engagement.

5. Ethical Vulnerability

A well-anchored value system supports ethical integrity, especially under pressure. Without it, educators may be more likely to make choices that compromise their character. For example, a teacher who values honesty will uphold grading standards, even when facing pressure from parents or administrators. But without a solid ethical foundation, there's a greater risk of cutting corners or rationalizing poor decisions. Over time, these compromises can erode self-respect, damage reputations, and weaken trust with students and peers.

6. Reduced Personal Growth

Values are the engine of continuous self-improvement. Educators with clearly defined values actively pursue opportunities for growth, both professionally and personally. For instance, a teacher who values *lifelong learning* may seek advanced certifications, participate in workshops, or engage in collaborative peer learning to enhance their skills. This inner drive keeps them inspired, sharp, and evolving with the demands of the profession. Without such motivation, however, educators risk stagnation. Over time, this can lead to dissatisfaction, a lack of progress, and, ultimately, disillusionment with their career.

7. Emotional Instability

Values provide an inner anchor—a stable foundation that helps educators stay grounded, especially during turbulent times. Without a clear set of values, educators may find themselves emotionally adrift, experiencing heightened stress, anxiety, or burnout. For example, a teacher facing a difficult classroom dynamic may feel overwhelmed if they lack guiding principles like *patience, empathy,* or *resilience*. When educators are grounded in their values, they're better equipped to respond rather than react, allowing them to navigate emotional challenges with greater confidence and composure.

Values' Influence on Educators

There is growing recognition that when students' *values*—that is, the things they consider personally important—are acknowledged and respected, the benefits ripple outward. Stronger relationships form. Academic engagement increases. Achievement improves. Overall well-being is enhanced (Hill et al., 2024).

On the flip side, when students' values are unmet, dismissed, or in conflict with their environment, they often disengage. This can lead to social withdrawal, a lack of purpose, and what some scholars refer to as "*illbeing*" (Schwartz, 2012; Sirgy, 2021; Tiberius, 2018). In other words, if we want students to flourish—not just function—in school, we must begin by understanding what they truly value.

Make no mistake: *values matter in education*. Acknowledging this truth allows educators to intentionally shape environments where students can thrive, not just academically, but personally and socially. While it may be tempting to dismiss "know your values" as soft or sentimental, in reality, values quietly run the show.

Teachers make dozens—often hundreds—of decisions daily, usually before their second cup of coffee. And most of those decisions? They're guided by personal values, whether consciously or not.

Values help educators choose how to respond, how to teach, and how to lead. In that sense, values aren't fluff—they're foundational.

Take, for example, the ever-divisive topic of school dress codes. If you've worked in a school for longer than ten minutes, you already know: the Great Hat Debate is alive and well. Some students wear hats like they're part of their identity, while certain teachers treat them like contraband. And administrators? They're just hoping to survive another week without a heated email thread about it.

Students often resist rules that feel arbitrary. Teachers differ in how strictly they enforce them. Administrators frequently lack the time—or the patience—for yet another staff meeting on the matter. On the surface, the teacher who rigidly enforces the dress code might be labeled inflexible or unsupportive of student autonomy. Conversely, the teacher who allows hats may be seen as lax or insubordinate. But when viewed through the lens of *core values*, a deeper understanding emerges.

The first teacher may prioritize *order*, *respect*, and *responsibility*, believing that structure fosters a productive and respectful environment. The second might value *freedom*, *self-expression*, and *trust*, believing that autonomy builds stronger student-teacher connections and a more authentic classroom culture. Understanding this helps bring clarity—and compassion—to conversations where perspectives differ.

Consider also the teacher who demands punctuality for every assignment versus the one who allows flexible deadlines. The first likely values *accountability* and *real-world readiness*; the second may prioritize *empathy* and *mental health*. Or look at the varied approaches to technology in the classroom: one teacher bans phones to support *focus* and *discipline*, while another integrates them to emphasize *engagement* and *relevance*.

Recognizing that these choices are grounded in personal values—not laziness, stubbornness, or inconsistency—can shift our conversations from judgment to understanding. This doesn't mean every teacher's personal values should dictate school-wide policy. But when educators and leaders acknowledge how values influence behavior, they open the door to more thoughtful dialogue. Instead of reacting with accusations, we begin to respond with curiosity.

This mindset creates a more collaborative and compassionate school culture—one in which diverse values aren't just tolerated but respected.

Values also influence the fabric of relationships and social dynamics within educational communities. When educators surround themselves with colleagues who share similar values, they build stronger social bonds, reinforce their *sense of purpose*, and foster a climate of mutual affirmation and motivation. These relationships become the emotional fuel that sustains long-term commitment and resilience.

However, in many schools, *values* are often overlooked, minimized, or pushed aside in favor of policies, test scores, and standardized outcomes. This neglect can lead to strained relationships, communication breakdowns, and missed opportunities to engage in meaningful dialogue about what truly drives educators.

It's also important to name a few common misconceptions about values in education—misunderstandings that often go unchallenged and prevent schools from fully embracing their transformative power. When we ignore these myths, we miss out on the deeper work of aligning our practices with what truly matters.

- **Misconception 1: Values Are Only Taught in Ethics or Moral Education Classes**

In reality, values are woven into every subject and every moment within the school environment. From teamwork on the soccer field to integrity during a math exam, values are modeled and reinforced all day long. Whether consciously or not, teachers impart values through their language, behavior, expectations, and relationships.

An art teacher guiding students to design a collaborative mural, or a music teacher helping students compose original songs, isn't just teaching technique—they're modeling *creativity, collaboration,* and *expression*. An

English teacher who encourages students to explore diverse perspectives through literature is fostering *open-mindedness* and *empathy*. These lessons are internalized not only through the curriculum but also by observing values being lived out in real time.

- **Misconception 2: Values Are Universal and Unchanging**

While core values like *honesty*, *fairness*, and *respect* are widely upheld, how they are understood and expressed can shift across cultures, communities, and generations. More importantly, values evolve.

A novice teacher may enter the classroom clinging to *structure* and *consistency* for survival. But after gaining experience and building deeper relationships, that same teacher may come to equally value *flexibility* and *creativity*. Likewise, a high-achieving student might initially prize *competition* and *achievement*, only to later discover that *collaboration*, *well-being*, or *purpose* matter more.

Schools are not static institutions. They are living ecosystems where values are taught, tested, transformed, and continually redefined.

- **Misconception 3: Schools Should Be Value-Neutral**

Some argue that schools should avoid influencing students' values altogether, clinging to the idea of neutrality. But education is never neutral. Every decision—whether about classroom management, grading policies, disciplinary practices, or curriculum choices—is inherently driven by *values*.

A school that implements zero-tolerance policies is operating from a different value framework than one that embraces *restorative justice*. A teacher who emphasizes *project-based learning* likely values *creativity*, *autonomy*, and *real-world application*, whereas one who prioritizes timed assessments might be grounded in *discipline*, *efficiency*, and *rigor*.

Rather than pretending that values don't exist in education, schools should acknowledge them openly, making those values visible, intentional, and aligned with their mission and community. Transparency about values doesn't indoctrinate students; it empowers them to reflect, question, and develop their own.

- **Misconception 4: Values Are Only About Right and Wrong**

It's easy to reduce values to moral binaries—right versus wrong, good versus bad. But many of the most essential values aren't about ethics at all—they're about personal growth, identity, and self-actualization.

Values like curiosity, perseverance, imagination, and adaptability are not about morality; they're about mindset. A student who values curiosity asks bold, thoughtful questions. A student who values perseverance keeps going after a failed science experiment or a tough math test. These values shape how learners approach challenges, solve problems, relate to others, and ultimately, how they see themselves in the world.

When educators limit values to "right vs. wrong," they miss the broader purpose: values help develop well-rounded human beings, not just rule followers.

- **Misconception 5: Values Are Only Relevant for Older Students**

Another common myth is that values education should be reserved for high school or college students—those old enough to "understand" character development. In truth, children begin forming and expressing values at a very young age.

A kindergartner shows *fairness* when they share a toy. A second grader demonstrates *honesty* when they admit to a mistake. A fourth grader practices *empathy* when they comfort a classmate. Waiting until students are older to explore values is a missed opportunity for *early social-emotional development*.

Educators at every level can integrate values meaningfully:

1. A first-grade teacher might use storybooks and classroom discussions to spark conversations about *kindness, inclusion,* or *respect.*
2. A fourth-grade class might co-create shared classroom norms rooted in values like *responsibility* and *teamwork.*
3. Middle school students can examine real-world ethical dilemmas, literature, or current events, and reflect on the *values in play.*

It's not about telling students what to value. It's about creating space—early and often—for them to *ask questions, reflect deeply, and explore what matters most to them.*

Discussion

- What universal values (if any) should all teachers teach?
- How should administrators assess a teacher's values before they are hired? (or should they?)
- What role should the Federal and State governments play in values education?
- In your educational experiences, are you more likely to discuss or not discuss values? Why?

Using Values to Navigate Education

In today's rapidly evolving educational landscape, where educators must navigate challenges such as technological advancements, diverse student needs, and shifting societal expectations, having a strong set of *values* is more critical than ever. *Values* serve as a guiding compass, shaping educators' decisions, actions, and interactions with students, colleagues, and the broader community. They are fundamental to fostering a learning environment that is both supportive and empowering, making them indispensable to the teaching profession.

Creating an Inclusive and Supportive Classroom

Core *values* such as *respect*, *integrity*, and *fairness* are essential in cultivating an inclusive and welcoming learning environment. *Respect* ensures that every student feels valued, heard, and understood, regardless of their background or abilities—an increasingly vital aspect of equitable education. *Integrity* compels educators to lead with honesty and ethical responsibility, setting an example for students to follow. *Fairness* guarantees that every learner is provided with equal opportunities to succeed, reinforcing the principle that education should be a level playing field. Together, these *values* build trust between teachers and students—a cornerstone of effective teaching and learning.

Navigating the Complexities of Modern Education

Educators who embrace *values* like *empathy* and *compassion* are better equipped to address the emotional and social needs of their students. In an era where mental health challenges among youth are increasingly prevalent, emotional well-being is just as important as academic achievement. By fostering supportive relationships and recognizing students' individual struggles, educators can create a safe and nurturing space where students feel encouraged to learn, grow, and thrive.

Commitment to Lifelong Learning and Growth

Values also play a critical role in educators' professional development. A commitment to *curiosity* and *lifelong learning* drives teachers to stay informed about new teaching methodologies, technological innovations, and best practices in education. This adaptability not only enhances their effectiveness in the classroom but also sets a powerful example for students, instilling in them a passion for continuous growth and learning.

Building a Collaborative and Accountable School Community

The *values* educators uphold extend well beyond the classroom walls, influencing how they collaborate with colleagues and contribute to the broader school community. A culture rooted in *collaboration* fosters teamwork, innovation, and shared problem-solving, while *accountability* ensures educators remain committed to delivering the highest quality education. By modeling these *values*, teachers reinforce the importance of *responsibility*, *cooperation*, and *shared success*—lessons that resonate far beyond academics and into life itself.

Preparing Students for a Globalized World

In an increasingly interconnected world, *values* such as *cultural awareness*, *openness*, and *adaptability* are crucial. Educators who prioritize these *values* prepare students to navigate a diverse society with *respect* and *understanding*. By fostering appreciation for different perspectives and backgrounds, teachers empower students to become informed, inclusive, and socially responsible global citizens.

The role of *values* in education cannot be overstated. They are not just personal guiding principles for educators—they shape the learning experience and influence students' academic, social, and emotional development. By embracing a strong set of *values*, educators elevate their impact, inspiring students to grow into *ethical, compassionate*, and *capable* individuals. Ultimately, education is about more than just imparting knowledge—it is about shaping the future by fostering a generation that leads with *integrity, respect*, and *purpose*.

Values, Beliefs, Desires, Wants, and Needs

Understanding the distinction between *core values, beliefs, desires, wants*, and *needs* is essential when exploring one's *purpose*. Each of these components plays a unique role and significantly affects how individuals perceive and pursue their goals, particularly in the field of education.

Core values are the fundamental ethical principles that guide behaviors and decision-making processes. These intrinsic and enduring *values*, such as *honesty, integrity*, and *compassion*, serve as the backbone of an individual's *purpose*, consistently influencing every aspect of life. For example, an educator who values *integrity* will ensure fairness in grading, while one who values *compassion* will strive to create an inclusive and supportive learning environment. These *values* shape not only personal actions but also interactions with students, colleagues, and the broader community.

Beliefs are convictions an individual holds to be true, ranging from religious doctrines to personal views about human nature and success. Examples include the belief that *hard work leads to success* or that *every student has the potential to learn given the right support.* While *core values* dictate ethical principles, *beliefs* are shaped by cultural, educational, and familial influences and can evolve over time based on experiences or new evidence. For instance, an educator who once believed in rigid discipline might shift their belief toward *student-centered learning* after seeing the positive impact of flexible teaching strategies.

Desires represent strong feelings of wanting to attain something or wishing for outcomes, such as *success, happiness,* or *recognition.* These are influenced by one's *core values* and *beliefs,* but are more transient and less foundational. For example, an educator might desire to be recognized with an award for outstanding teaching, which aligns with a *core value* of *excellence.* However, *desires* can change based on circumstances, and unlike *values*, they are not always essential for fulfillment.

Wants and *needs*, though related to *desires*, differ in their level of necessity. *Wants* are non-essential items or experiences individuals would like to have, such as a *luxury car* or an *exotic vacation.* They reflect personal preferences and lifestyle choices but are not fundamental to well-being. In contrast, *needs* are essential for survival and basic functioning, such as *food, shelter,* and emotional connections like *love* and *support.* For example, an educator might want a *state-of-the-art classroom* with advanced technology, but their actual need is simply a *functional space* conducive to learning. *Needs* are non-negotiable and must be met for individuals to thrive, while *wants* can be adjusted or deferred.

The interrelation among *core values, beliefs, desires, wants,* and *needs* significantly impacts an individual's decisions and life direction. By aligning these factors, an educator can gain a clearer understanding of their *purpose* and make decisions that lead to a more fulfilling career and life. For instance, a teacher who values *lifelong learning* (core value), believes in *continuous professional development* (belief), desires to *earn an advanced degree* (desire), wants to *attend a prestigious conference* (want), and needs *financial stability* (need) can make strategic choices that align with their overarching goals.

This alignment not only provides direction but also fosters fulfillment and satisfaction in pursuing goals that resonate deeply with one's ethical and personal standards. Introspection and alignment of *core values, beliefs, desires, wants,* and *needs* are essential for discovering and fulfilling one's *purpose,* reinforcing the importance of understanding how each component shapes one's life trajectory.

Guiding Light: Next Steps

Are you a school leader? Then you're in a unique position to not only shape school culture, but to shape it with *intention*. One of the most powerful ways to do this is by creating space for educators to reflect on their personal *values* and how those *values* influence everything, from instructional choices to hallway conversations. When teachers are clear about what they stand for—whether it's *rigor, curiosity, compassion, or perseverance*—they bring greater clarity and consistency to their work. These *values* become a lens for decision-making and a foundation for relationships with students, families, and colleagues.

Start by carving out time for meaningful reflection. Faculty meetings, professional development days, or even beginning-of-year retreats are great opportunities to introduce tools like the *Personal Values Audit* (Appendix A)—a simple but powerful resource that helps educators identify and articulate their core values. But don't stop at identification. Invite *discussion:*

- *How do your values show up in your classroom?*
- *What happens when they're challenged?*
- *How can we support one another in living them out?*

When school leaders make *values* visible—not just in mission statements, but in everyday modeling and conversations—they give permission for others to do the same. The result? A culture where *alignment* matters more than *compliance,* where difficult decisions become clearer, and where educators feel more grounded, motivated, and connected to their *"why."* Because when *values* are front and center, school becomes more than a workplace—it becomes a *purpose-driven community*.

As a leader, share how your *values* influence your actions:

- *I value transparency, so I want to walk you through why we're making this schedule change.*
- *I believe in shared leadership, which is why I want your input before finalizing the new grading policy. Your voices matter in shaping how we serve our students.*
- *I've learned from experience that feedback helps us grow. I might not always get it right the first time, but I'm committed to learning and evolving, just like we ask of our students.*
- *I believe leaders should be accountable, too. If this decision doesn't have the impact we hope, I'll take responsibility, and we'll adjust together.*

Are you a teacher? Then you already know—you do so much more than deliver content. You model character, build community, and help shape the lens through which your students see the world. One powerful way to deepen that impact is by helping students explore their personal **values.** These lesson plans (Appendix B) are designed to spark meaningful conversations and reflections about what truly matters to each learner. Whether it's fairness, creativity, kindness, or perseverance, understanding one's values builds self-awareness, connection, and motivation—skills that last far beyond the final bell.

Classroom Lessons

But it starts with *you*. Regardless of your role in education, you can live by your *values* daily, and your students will notice. When you make decisions, give feedback, or manage challenges through the lens of your *values*, you model *integrity in action*. It's one thing to say *"respect matters"*—it's another to show it consistently through *tone, timing,* and *trust*.

Bring your colleagues into the conversation, too. Talking about *values* isn't fluff—it's foundational. Imagine a school where educators regularly reflect on how their *values* shape interactions with students, families, and one another. The result? Stronger relationships, more consistent classroom cultures, and a community grounded in shared *humanity*.

So, dive into these lessons. Ask your students what they *believe in*, what *lights them up*, and what they *want to stand for*. Reflect on your own *values*, share them out loud, and invite others to do the same. Because when *values* are visible, school becomes more than a place to learn—it becomes a place to *grow as people*.

In the ever-evolving journey of education, *values* are more than words on a poster—they are the invisible threads that weave together *purpose, passion*, and *practice*. When educators lead with their *values*, they illuminate the path not just for themselves, but for every student they encounter. They create classrooms where *trust* and *genuine connection* thrive, where *learning* is fueled by *curiosity*, and where *challenges* become catalysts for *growth*. In a world that often demands quick answers and easy fixes, *values* remind us to *pause, reflect*, and *act with intention*. They are our *steady ground* in uncertain times and our *compass* when the way forward seems unclear.

As you continue your journey—as a *teacher*, a *learner*, or a *leader*—may your *values* guide you boldly, may your *purpose* burn brightly, and may the *impact* you leave behind echo far beyond the walls of any classroom.

Values Development Checklist for All School Personnel

Use this checklist to reflect on how well you're supporting the development of values in yourself, your students, and your colleagues. Check all that apply.

Promoting Values Awareness and Alignment

- I regularly reflect on my own core values and how they show up in my daily actions.

- I help students identify what values are important to them.
- I create opportunities for students and staff to connect values to their goals and decisions.
- I notice when actions are misaligned with values and take steps to correct them.

Fostering Purpose and Meaning

- I support students and colleagues in exploring how values contribute to meaningful goals.
- I connect classroom learning to real-world purpose and personal relevance.
- I share my "why" as an educator and encourage others to do the same.
- I remind students that strong values can help them persevere through challenges.

Encouraging Integrity and Authenticity

- I model integrity, even when it's difficult or inconvenient.
- I encourage others to act in ways that reflect their values.
- I foster an environment where people feel safe being their authentic selves.
- I recognize and celebrate moments when students and staff express their true selves and act in alignment with their values.

Creating a Values-Based Culture

- I talk about values in everyday conversations, lessons, or meetings.
- I help create shared expectations around respect, kindness, and responsibility.
- I acknowledge and honor the diverse values and backgrounds of others.
- I encourage values-based decision-making in our school community.

Voices from the Field

Chris: As a kindergarten teacher, my classroom is built on three magical values: kindness, patience, and curiosity. These aren't just words on a poster—they're the heartbeat of everything we do! Kindness is our superpower. Whether it's sharing crayons, giving a high-five, or helping a friend zip their coat, we practice it every day. I work hard to make sure every child feels safe, seen, and deeply loved. We talk about feelings, celebrate differences, and learn how to be gentle with each other's hearts.

Patience? Oh yes—it's my secret sidekick. In our classroom, we know that everyone grows at their own speed. Some kids zip through the alphabet, while others are still figuring out where "Q" goes—and that's okay! I cheer on every tiny victory like it's a parade, because progress is worth celebrating, big or small.

And curiosity? That's the sparkle in our day! Whether we're wondering how caterpillars turn into butterflies or what happens when you mix blue and yellow, I follow my students' questions wherever they lead. I want them to see the world as a place full of wonder, just waiting to be explored.

At the end of the day, I teach because I want to help little humans grow into kind, confident, and curious big ones. And it all starts right here, in our joyful, wiggly, love-filled classroom.

Ezra: As an industrial arts teacher, my core values—integrity, craftsmanship, and perseverance—guide everything I do in the classroom. I believe in the dignity of hard work and the importance of creating something meaningful with your hands. That belief shapes the way I teach. I emphasize attention to detail, pride in your work, and learning through doing.

I value being genuine and real with students, and that comes through in how I interact with them. I'm honest, I hold them accountable, and I show them that mistakes are part of the learning process. In my shop, effort matters just as much as the outcome. I want students to know their work has value, not just the final product, but the mindset and persistence it takes to get there. Respect is another value I model daily—respect for tools, for safety, for one another, and for the craft itself.

I strive to create an environment where students take ownership, solve problems, and develop confidence through hands-on experience. My goal isn't just to teach them how to use equipment—it's to help them develop a work ethic, a sense of pride, and skills they can carry with them for life.

References

Beck, C. (1990). *Better Schools: A Values Perspective.* Falmer Press, Taylor & Francis, Inc., 1900 Frost Road, Suite 101, Bristol, PA 19007.

Harter, S. (2002). Authenticity. In C. R. Snyder & S. J. Lopez (Eds.), *Handbook of positive psychology* (pp. 382–394). Oxford University Press.

Halstead, M. (2005). Values and values education in schools. In *Values in education and education in values* (pp. 3-14). Routledge.

Hill, J. L., van Driel, J., Seah, W. T., & Kern, M. L. (2024). Students' values in science education: a scoping review. *Studies in Science Education*, 1–53. https://doi.org/10.1080/03057267.2024.2412456

Matthes, E. (Ed.). (2004). *Werteorientierter Unterricht-eine Herausforderung für die Schulfächer.* Auer.

Ofsted. (2019). School inspection handbook.

Schwartz, S. H. (2012). An overview of the Schwartz theory of basic values. *Online Readings in Psychology and Culture*, 2(1). https://doi.org/10.9707/2307-0919.1116

Sirgy, M. J. (2021). Effects of beliefs and values on well-being. In M. J. Sirgy (Ed.), *The psychology of quality of life* (pp. 245–262). Springer. https://doi.org/10.1007/978-3-030-71888-6_11

Tiberius, V. (2018). *Well-being as value fulfillment: How we can help each other to live well.* Oxford University Press.

03 | Purpose Powered by Passion:

Living Your Values Out Loud

Passion is energy. Feel the power that comes from focusing on what excites you.

— **Oprah Winfrey**

> Passions are feelings of intense enthusiasm and excitement for something. They are often the inspiration behind an individual's motivation and energy. Passions propel a person to pursue activities, careers, or causes that they find deeply fulfilling and enjoyable. When an educator aligns their life's work or activities with their passions, they are more likely to experience a strong sense of satisfaction and purpose.

Just as values shape who we are, passions illuminate what energizes us, revealing the unique paths we are meant to follow. Think about how you feel when engaging in something you're truly *passionate* about—whether it's mentoring students, coaching a team, gardening, writing, or building something with your hands. Words like *excitement, joy, flow,* and *energy* often emerge. You might even forget to eat lunch or pick up your kids. Now, contrast that with an activity disconnected from your *passions*. You may feel *boredom, dread,* or simply a desire to *"get it over with."* You might even mindlessly eat or daydream about the day you don't have to pick up your kids! That emotional contrast highlights how central *passion* is to shaping our experiences and perspective.

Passion is the intense *enthusiasm* and *excitement* for something. It is often the driving force behind an individual's motivation and energy. *Passion* propels a person to pursue activities, careers, or causes that they find deeply fulfilling and enjoyable. It's a deep, sustaining force that gives meaning to our actions. *Passion* fuels our desire to pursue *excellence*, *persevere* through challenges, and find *fulfillment* in both the process and the outcome. This intense enthusiasm is the reason people wake up early for workouts, stay late to finish projects, or debate grammar rules in group chats. *Intrinsic motivation* helps turn obstacles into opportunities and challenges into growth experiences. When an educator aligns their life's work or activities with their *passions*, they are more likely to experience a strong sense of *satisfaction* and *purpose*. When harnessed, it becomes a catalyst for *personal growth* and *meaningful contributions*.

When people pursue their *passions*—whether it's inventing eco-tech, choreographing musicals, or launching nonprofits from their garage—they do more than chase dreams. They make society *brighter, bolder,* and a heck of a lot more interesting. *Passion* fuels *innovation, art,* and *social change*. It's why we have *jazz, peaceful protests,* and people who genuinely enjoy organizing spreadsheets. *Passion* pulls others in, sparks *action*, and occasionally leads to accidentally ordering art projects online at 2 a.m. Even if it's not Nobel Prize-level, *passion* still matters. It's the *barista* making foam hearts, the *teacher* staying late for a student, and the *neighbor* with endless door decorations. These moments add *joy* and *meaning* to the world. When people do what they love, *everyone benefits*. We get better ideas, stronger connections, and maybe even a new genre of donut. *Passion* is what keeps the world moving forward—and makes the ride way more fun.

Often, *passion* is rooted in our *values*—core beliefs that guide our choices. When we align our work with both our *passions* and *values*, we experience greater *fulfillment* and *consistency*. Someone *passionate* about *conservation* may thrive in advocacy roles. That alignment keeps them *committed*, even when the work gets tough. For educators, this alignment is especially powerful. Teaching with *passion* brings energy into the classroom, ignites curiosity, and fosters lifelong learning. Think of a teacher who *lights up* when discussing physics or the PE teacher who *runs laps* with her students. Without *passion*, even the best-planned lessons can feel disengaging.

Passionate educators are the heartbeat of dynamic schools. They spark *curiosity*, *inspire* students, and build *authentic relationships*. They foster deep, meaningful connections with students and colleagues, contributing to a culture of *trust* and *collaboration*. School communities that actively nurture the *passions* of their staff and students often see greater *morale*, *engagement*, and *academic success*.

Ultimately, for educators, *passion* is not just a personal asset—it is a powerful tool for shaping the future. It breathes life into classrooms, nurtures curiosity, and builds meaningful relationships. An educator's *passion* is the essential driving force behind their teaching *purpose*, acting as a catalyst for significant impact in the educational landscape. This emotional drive fuels their *enthusiasm* and *creativity*, inspiring student engagement with an infectious energy and excitement about the subject matter. *Passionate* educators not only encourage students to delve beyond surface-level learning but also promote *curiosity* and *critical thinking* by urging them to ask questions, explore new ideas, and engage in deep thinking.

Their *passion* fosters meaningful relationships with students, reflecting a *genuine interest* in their personal growth and well-being. It is crucial in overcoming various educational challenges—including *limited resources*, *behavioral issues*, and *policy changes*—by equipping educators with the *clarity* and *strength* needed to navigate these obstacles effectively.

The Power of Passion in Teaching and Learning

Teachers who bring this energy into the classroom transform learning into a shared journey. Their excitement is contagious. When teachers express genuine enthusiasm for a subject, it signals to students that learning is not just important—it's *exhilarating*. This emotional contagion often leads to increased student participation, curiosity, and motivation. In classrooms where this energy is present, both students and staff develop a positive emotional connection to learning.

Consider the influence of a history teacher who reenacts pivotal moments, tells captivating stories, or shares authentic historical artifacts. Suddenly, history is no longer a timeline of dates and events—it becomes a *living narrative*. Or the art teacher who turns their classroom into a laboratory of *creativity*, encouraging *expression* and *exploration*. These displays of *passion*, however, are not just reserved for classroom teachers. We all know those amazing custodians who not only take *pride* in their work but also share this pride with students. Or the school administrative assistant who shows up for all the school plays and fundraisers. These are small but *significant* displays of *passion*.

Passion is *magnetic* and *necessary* for learning. A student who is genuinely *passionate* about a topic transcends *rote memorization* and *standardized testing*. Instead, they seek to *understand, question*, and *connect* ideas in meaningful ways. As Jachimowicz et al. (2018) insightfully noted, *"Perseverance without passion is mere drudgery, but perseverance with passion propels individuals forward."* This dynamic blend of *persistence* and *passion*—commonly known as *grit*—equips individuals to thrive even in the face of adversity.

Student *engagement*—so essential to academic success—flourishes under the guidance of *passionate* educators. Engagement is most powerful when students are not passive consumers of information but *active participants* in their own learning journey. Teachers who infuse their instruction with *passion* often incorporate *project-based learning, real-world applications*, and *student-driven inquiry*.

A literature teacher might give students the option to analyze a novel through an essay, a podcast, or a short film—empowering them to choose the medium that resonates most with their interests and strengths. An art teacher might work with students to paint a mural over graffiti, transforming abstract concepts into *lived experiences*. In these classrooms, students are more than learners—they are *co-creators* of knowledge.

Passionate educators foster this environment by posing *thought-provoking questions*, integrating *student interests* into the curriculum, and making meaningful connections between academic content and students' lives, cultures, and aspirations. *Passion* is not a luxury in education—it is a *necessity*. It transforms the *ordinary* into the *extraordinary*, lights the path to *deeper understanding*, and cultivates *lifelong learners* prepared not just to absorb knowledge, but to *apply it with purpose and creativity*.

Video

Reflection

Video

- What excites you about a career in education?
- How do you share your passions with students and colleagues?
- What passion do you wish you had more time to pursue?
- What do you feel when you think about something you are passionate about?
- How can educators help students discover their passions?

Connecting Hearts and Minds: The Role of Passion in Student-Teacher Relationships

Strong student-teacher relationships are the foundation of an enriching and impactful educational experience. Poulou (2017) found that the teacher-student relationship in the classroom is essential for academic success. At the heart of these relationships lies *passion*—not only for the subject matter, but for teaching itself and for nurturing each student as a whole person. When educators are *passionate*, they create more than just a classroom—they build a *community* where students feel *seen*, *valued*, and *inspired*. Research by Pianta, Hamre, and Allen (2012) emphasizes that positive teacher-student interactions are critical for promoting student *engagement* and *achievement*.

Video

Just as important as the content is the relationship *passionate* educators build with their students. According to Roorda et al. (2011), positive student-teacher relationships significantly impact *academic engagement* and *emotional well-being*. When students feel *safe*, *understood*, and *supported*, they are more likely to take *intellectual risks*, participate actively, and persevere through challenges. *Passionate* educators are often the ones who take time to ask, *"How are you doing today?"* or who adapt an assignment when they notice a student struggling, not to lower expectations, but to better align support with the student's needs. These educators go beyond the curriculum. They learn about their students' *interests*, *challenges*, and *dreams*.

Passionate Teachers
1. A math teacher who discovers a student's love for art might incorporate geometric patterns and design into a lesson, bridging personal interest with academic content.
2. A biology teacher might stay after class to support a student passionate about marine life, sharing documentaries or research opportunities to encourage deeper exploration.
3. In an elementary classroom, a kindergarten teacher noticing that a student loves dinosaurs might create a counting activity using dinosaur figurines to teach addition and subtraction.
4. A third-grade teacher might learn that a shy student enjoys

drawing and allow them to illustrate a story instead of writing it, helping them build confidence in their own way.

Personalized connections make learning *relevant* and *engaging*, and show students that their teachers care about *who they are* as individuals. These seemingly small gestures establish *trust* and send a powerful

Video

message: *I care about more than your grade—I care about your growth.* This kind of genuine, personal investment can be especially powerful for students who may feel overlooked or disconnected.

A middle school student struggling with behavior issues might begin to thrive after a teacher consistently checks in, listens without judgment, and helps them set *personal goals*. At the elementary level, imagine a kindergartner who often acts out during group time. A *passionate* teacher, instead of punishing the child, might take a moment during recess to sit beside them and ask, *"What's been hard for you today?"* That small act of care might uncover that the child is feeling overwhelmed or left out—insight that helps the teacher better support and guide them moving forward.

Creating a *supportive* and *inclusive* classroom is essential to cultivating these meaningful relationships. *Passionate* educators intentionally create environments where students feel emotionally safe, respected, and encouraged to take risks. In such spaces, *diversity of thought* is celebrated, *mistakes* are reframed as learning opportunities, and students feel empowered to speak their minds.

Confidence-building is another hallmark of strong student-teacher relationships. *Passionate* teachers act as *mentors* and *advocates*, helping students see potential in themselves that they may not yet recognize. Consider a science teacher who notices a student's analytical strengths and encourages them to enter a local STEM competition. The student, initially uncertain, rises to the occasion, gains recognition, and begins to envision a future they hadn't previously considered. That single act of encouragement can alter a student's trajectory.

In elementary school, a teacher might notice that a second grader has a knack for public speaking. Instead of simply having them read aloud in class, the teacher encourages them to lead the morning announcements or represent the class at a school assembly. That small boost of responsibility can light a spark, showing the student they have something *special* to offer, and helping them believe in their own *capabilities*.

Moreover, when students feel emotionally connected to their teachers, they are more likely to take *intellectual risks*, ask *questions*, and engage with the material at a deeper level. They begin to internalize the belief that they are *capable* and *worthy of success*. As a result, *academic outcomes* improve—but so do essential *life skills*: *cooperation, communication, self-awareness,* and *critical thinking*. Ultimately, passion-driven relationships between students and teachers do more than enhance classroom engagement—they shape *character*, inspire *confidence*, and foster a *lifelong love of learning*. These connections are the *unseen architecture* of educational success. They remind us that great teaching isn't just about transferring knowledge—it's about *touching lives*.

Discussion

- What role and responsibility do educators have for tapping into student passions?
- How can administrators support teacher passions?
- What do you feel helps students and teachers find and pursue their passions?
- Is it true that some people are just more passionate about everything than others? Explain.

Sharing and supporting student passions is not the sole responsibility of classroom teachers. Every adult in a school community—*teachers, counselors, coaches, support staff,* and *administrators*—can play a role in nurturing *purpose* and *passion*. When school leaders actively create space for both teachers and students to explore what excites them, it sets a tone that values *curiosity, creativity,* and *connection*.

Supporting *passion* doesn't always mean creating new programs—it can be as simple as *listening closely*, *encouraging exploration*, or *connecting students with opportunities beyond the classroom.*

For example, school leaders can support passion by:

Spotlighting a teacher's talent:

A principal discovers that the fifth-grade science teacher is an avid beekeeper. They help the teacher set up a small apiary on campus, weaving bee-hive maintenance into science, math, and environmental stewardship lessons for multiple grade levels.

Food Science Video

Elevating student voice:

During cafeteria duty, the principal notices several middle-schoolers trading homemade comic strips. Recognizing their enthusiasm, the principal creates a lunchtime *"Graphic Novel Studio,"* pairing the students with the art and English departments to publish a quarterly anthology sold at school events.

Expanding community connections:

After learning that a parent volunteer is a professional chef passionate about healthy eating, the principal invites them to co-launch a *"Farm-to-Table"* program. Together, they introduce seasonal tasting days, garden-to-kitchen demos, and nutrition workshops that align with health-class standards.

Empowering staff leadership:

A math coach who loves robotics shares a weekend competition video with the principal. Seeing the potential, the principal reallocates discretionary funds to start a schoolwide *robotics league*, positioning the coach as the program's coordinator and mentoring other teachers to integrate coding challenges into their curricula.

Building school culture through the arts:

When teachers mention a custodian's passion for drumming, the principal arranges for them to lead *morning rhythm circles*. These daily five-minute routines boost attendance and provide a unifying ritual that transitions students smoothly from arrival to class.

The old saying *"it takes a village"* may feel overused, but in the context of education, it couldn't be truer. Creating a culture where student *passions* are recognized and supported requires the collective commitment of an *entire school community*. When every adult takes ownership of nurturing *purpose*—regardless of their role—students thrive not just academically, but as *whole, inspired* individuals.

Dynamic Learning: Adjusting Strategies for Student Success

Passionate educators understand that learning is not a one-size-fits-all journey. It is deeply *personal*, shaped by each student's *strengths, struggles, backgrounds*, and *pace*. Exceptional teachers recognize these differences and are *intentional* about tailoring their instructional approach to support every learner. They remain *observant* and *empathetic*, ready to pivot, encourage, and adjust to create the best possible learning environment.

For instance, a *passionate* teacher may notice that a once-enthusiastic student has become quiet or distracted. Rather than assuming disengagement, the teacher might take a moment to check in privately, ask how the student is feeling, and offer support, be it *academic, emotional*, or even just a *listening ear*. These seemingly small interactions can make a major difference, fostering a culture of *care, trust*, and *accountability* that benefits the entire classroom community.

Truly *dynamic teaching* requires *adaptability*. *Passionate* educators understand that every classroom has its own *energy, learning styles*, and *challenges*. They are not rigid in their delivery—they adjust, evolve, and refine based on their students' needs. This might involve shifting from lecture-style teaching to *group projects*, incorporating *visual aids* and *audio clips* for auditory and visual learners, or bringing in *real-world connections* to deepen understanding.

A chemistry teacher might realize that many students are struggling to grasp molecular bonding through lectures and notes. Instead of continuing down the same path, the teacher introduces a *lab-based activity* where students use model kits to physically build molecules. The visual and tactile experience helps abstract concepts *click*, and the classroom comes alive with *collaboration* and *"aha" moments*.

For elementary students, a third-grade teacher might notice students zoning out during a lesson on the water cycle. In response, the teacher transitions to a *hands-on experiment* where students build mini water cycles using plastic containers and lamps. Suddenly, the room buzzes with *curiosity* and *engagement*.

Flexibility also means valuing *feedback*, not just from test scores or performance data, but from *student voice*. *Passionate* educators create *open lines of communication* where students feel safe offering input about what works for them and what doesn't. Some teachers use *anonymous surveys* or *exit tickets* to gather quick insights, while others build time into class for *reflection* and *suggestions*.

This might involve distributing a quick survey asking students which elements of a novel unit they enjoyed most—class discussions, Socratic seminars, creative writing assignments, or group presentations. When students see their feedback influencing future assignments (e.g., more student-led discussions or creative alternatives to essays), they feel *respected* and more *invested* in the learning process.

Moreover, *passionate* educators are tuned into moments when a lesson isn't landing. Rather than pressing forward, they pause, reassess, and reimagine. If a history unit on explorers isn't connecting, the teacher might ditch the textbook for a student-created *"Explorer Passport Project,"* where each student takes on the role of an explorer and presents their findings in a creative way.

In a high school civics class, a teacher may notice students disengaging from a lecture on the legislative process. Instead of continuing with slides, the teacher introduces a *mock congress simulation* where students take on roles as senators and representatives. Suddenly, students are debating bills, forming coalitions, and experiencing democracy in action. That shift turns *passive learning* into a *meaningful, immersive* experience.

Video

Dynamic learning is not about grand, complicated changes. Often, it's the *simple, thoughtful adjustments* that make the biggest impact—responding to energy levels with *movement breaks*, offering *flexible seating* for fidgety learners, or modifying assignments to match students' strengths.

What defines a *passionate* educator is their *commitment* to meeting students where they are and guiding them forward with *compassion, creativity,* and *intention*. In the end, this *responsiveness* transforms education from a one-way transmission of knowledge into a vibrant, *two-way exchange,* where students are not passive recipients but *active, enthusiastic participants* in their own learning journey.

Catalysts of Curiosity: The Enduring Influence of Passionate Educators

Passionate educators possess a transformative power—one that turns even the most disengaged students into *curious, active participants* in their learning. Their energy is not merely present; it's *palpable*. By infusing their classrooms with *authentic enthusiasm,* they create a dynamic learning environment where *curiosity* is not just encouraged but expected. Research by Frenzel et al. (2009) found that students are more *motivated* and *perform better* when their teachers exhibit enthusiasm, suggesting that *teacher affect* is a powerful contributor to *classroom climate* and *engagement*.

Their deep investment in both *content* and *student growth* fosters a culture where learning becomes an *adventure,* not a *task*. Rather than relying on traditional methods that emphasize *rote memorization,* these educators spark *intellectual exploration*. They engage students through *thought-provoking questions, interactive experiences,* and *real-world connections*. In doing so, they cultivate *critical thinking* and *problem-solving* skills that extend far beyond the classroom. Research supports this approach: when students are invited to engage in *meaningful inquiry,* they develop a stronger sense of *ownership* and *motivation* for learning (Ryan & Deci, 2000).

Just as essential as *instructional creativity* is the *relational foundation* that *passionate* educators build with their students. These relationships are the cornerstone of a *safe, inclusive* learning environment—spaces where students feel *known, respected,* and *supported*. According to Roorda et al. (2011), *positive teacher-student relationships* are a significant predictor of *academic engagement* and *achievement*.

Passionate educators recognize that when students feel *emotionally connected* to their teachers, they are more willing to take *risks*, ask *questions*, and persist through *challenges*.

They also personalize learning by adapting to the *unique strengths* and *needs* of their students. A teacher who notices a student struggling with written assignments might offer alternatives like *podcasts* or *visual presentations*. A student who feels unseen in a large classroom might blossom under the care of a teacher who makes time for *regular check-ins*. These *intentional acts of support* reinforce students' *self-worth* and help them realize their *potential*.

Ultimately, the influence of *passionate* educators extends far beyond *academic outcomes*. They nurture *curiosity*, build *confidence*, and equip students with the *skills* to thrive in an *ever-changing world*. Their legacy is written not only in *test scores*, but in the *lives they shape*—the *thinkers, creators,* and *leaders* who carry their *passion* forward.

Overcoming Challenges with Resilience: How Passion Helps Educators Navigate Obstacles

Passion in education serves as a guiding light for educators, enabling them to navigate the myriad *challenges* that arise in their profession with *resilience* and *determination*. In a field often marked by *systemic limitations, evolving expectations,* and *emotional labor, passionate* educators find strength in their *purpose*. Rather than being discouraged by challenges, they view them as *opportunities* for *growth, innovation,* and *deeper connection* with their students.

Resilient teachers understand that obstacles—whether they be *limited funding, diverse learning needs,* or *institutional pressure*—are part of the job. But what sets *passionate* educators apart is their *mindset.* They respond with *creativity* and *commitment.*

For instance, a teacher facing resource shortages might partner with *local businesses,* apply for *grants,* or repurpose *everyday materials* to create *hands-on learning experiences.* These efforts do more than fill gaps—they model *problem-solving, adaptability,* and *perseverance* for their students.

Equally important is the *emotional resilience* that *passion* nurtures. Educators often serve as *first responders* to their students' emotional needs. *Passionate* teachers willingly go beyond academics—they *listen, mentor,* and *advocate.* Whether staying after school to help a struggling student or adjusting a lesson to accommodate a learner's unique circumstances, they provide a level of *care* that builds *trust* and *motivates* students to keep going, even when life gets hard.

Moreover, passionate educators are not immune to setbacks, but they refuse to be defined by them. They reflect, regroup, and persist. This model of resilience is invaluable to students, especially those facing their own struggles. When students witness a teacher's determination in the face of adversity, they internalize the message that challenges are not endpoints—they're opportunities to rise.

In essence, passion is both the spark and the sustaining flame in education. It empowers teachers to lead with heart, adapt with purpose, and inspire with integrity. Their resilience doesn't just carry them through tough times—it transforms their classrooms into spaces of possibility and promise, where both educators and students thrive.

Strategies to Spark and Sustain Passion at School

Teachers Supporting Student Passion	Principals Supporting Teacher Passion
Create "Passion Hour" or "Genius Time" – Give students dedicated time to explore personal interests	Provide Autonomy in Curriculum Design – Trust teachers to adapt content in ways that energize them
Co-create Learning Goals – Invite students to help shape objectives and outcomes	Allocate Time for Professional Learning – Build in time for learning during the school day
Use Project-Based Learning – Center lessons around solving meaningful, real-world problems	Offer Flexible Scheduling – Provide planning days, late starts, or mental health afternoons
Gamify Lessons – Turn lessons into games, challenges, or competitions to re-engage learners	Recognize and Celebrate Strengths – Use newsletters, shout-outs, or awards to highlight great teaching
Offer Student Choice – Let students pick how they show what they know (e.g., videos, songs, essays)	Encourage Innovation and Risk-Taking – Support teachers trying new methods without fear of "failing"
Bring in Experts or Community Members – Help students connect learning to real careers and people	Create Teacher-Led Teams and Initiatives – Empower teachers to lead committees or passion projects
Incorporate Movement and Outdoor Time – Let students learn in non-traditional spaces	Host Wellness and Reflection Activities – Provide yoga, journaling, or mindfulness PD sessions
Use Student Passions in Lessons – Integrate pop culture, hobbies, or music into core content	Facilitate Peer Collaboration – Encourage teacher PLCs or cross-subject planning groups
Celebrate Effort and Creativity, Not Just Accuracy – Shift focus from perfection to persistence	Support Career Growth – Fund conferences, offer leadership pathways, and mentor aspiring leaders
Model Passion – Share what excites you: your love for history, your favorite book, or fun hobbies	Ask for Teacher Feedback—and Act on It – Involve staff in decisions to keep morale and buy-in strong

It is imperative to move forward; we must understand that the absence of passion is a signal, not a dead end. It offers an invitation to pause, reflect, and explore. It's a detour sign. Maybe you reconnect with old loves—art, music, activism—or discover new ones, like coaching debate or leading a gardening club. Whether it leads to new discoveries or a rekindling of old interests, the journey to rediscover passion can be transformative. It opens the door to renewed engagement, a stronger sense of identity, and a clearer, more inspired path forward. Lost passion is often the catalyst for reinvention, not resignation. Sometimes, losing your spark is exactly what leads you to a bigger fire.

Driven by Values: Igniting Passion for a Purposeful Life

Passion and *values* are inextricably linked, forming the foundation of a *meaningful* and *purpose-driven* life. *Passion* often emerges from *deeply held values*—it is the *emotional current* that propels individuals toward pursuits aligned with their *core beliefs*. When people act in *harmony* with their values, their work becomes more than a task; it transforms into a *personal mission*. Someone who treasures *creativity* may feel most alive in artistic endeavors, while a person committed to *service* may find deep fulfillment in education, healthcare, or social work. Or, if you're like that one friend who organizes their sock drawer by *color-coded mood categories*, maybe your *passion* lies in logistics and precision. This alignment infuses life with *coherence, genuine purpose,* and a *sense of wholeness*.

The strength of this connection is evident in the way *passion* motivates *sustained, purposeful action*. When individuals engage in work that reflects their *values*, they tend to experience greater *motivation, adaptability,* and *long-term satisfaction*. This alignment fosters a reinforcing cycle: pursuing *passion* deepens one's connection to their *values*, and those *values* continue to fuel that *passion*. Those who care deeply about *fairness, inclusion,* and the *growth of young minds* often experience their profession not just as a job, but as a *mission*. Their *purpose* drives them to innovate, support, and lead in ways that go far beyond *"please put your name on your paper."*

Moreover, recognizing the connection between *values* and *passion* can shape both *career paths* and *personal growth*. Clarity around one's *values* offers a *template for decision-making*, helping individuals identify what truly excites and fulfills them. It's the reason someone might turn down a *six-figure job in finance* to open a bakery that specializes in *gluten-free cupcakes shaped like sea creatures*—because *fulfillment tastes better than money*. This *self-awareness* allows for more *intentional choices* about careers, relationships, and creative pursuits. Aligning *professional endeavors* with *personal values* cultivates a sense of *integrity* and *joy*, key ingredients for *long-term fulfillment and success*.

This connection also plays a *vital role* in building *perseverance*. *Challenges are inevitable*, but individuals who are driven by *values-based passion* are more likely to view obstacles as *meaningful hurdles* rather than roadblocks. Their *inner compass* helps them stay *grounded* and *focused*, even in times of uncertainty. A nonprofit leader who values *social justice*, for example, may face numerous external challenges, but their *belief in their cause* provides the *fortitude to persist*. In this way, *passion* rooted in *values* acts as an *emotional anchor* during life's storms.

The synergy between *passion* and *values* not only shapes how individuals live but also how they *lead* and *influence others*. People who live in *alignment* with their *values* often *radiate purpose*, attracting and inspiring those around them. They model what it means to lead a life of *substance*, where *impact, integrity*, and *fulfillment* intersect. Their example can foster a *ripple effect*, encouraging others to reflect on their own *passions* and *values* and to pursue more intentional, values-driven lives.

In a world that often prioritizes *performance over purpose*, nurturing the bond between *passion* and *values* is essential. It is through this connection that individuals find *clarity* in their goals, *adaptability* in their struggles, and *meaning* in their everyday actions. Understanding this link is not just a personal insight—it is a *powerful strategy* for building a more *empathetic, purposeful,* and *inspired* society.

Living Out Loud: Next Steps

Are you a school leader? Then you have the incredible opportunity to ignite *passion* not just in your students, but in the educators who guide them every day. One powerful way to do that is by providing *intentional space* for teachers to reflect on their *passions*—what fuels them, excites them, and keeps them going even on the busiest, most chaotic days. Ask questions like: *What brings you the most joy in your role? What parts of your job do you lose track of time doing?* These aren't just warm-and-fuzzy prompts—they're essential insights into how educators show up in the classroom and connect with students.

Activity

Tools like the *Passions Audit* (Appendix C) can support this exploration, helping teachers identify not only their professional drivers but also the *values* that anchor them. When leaders make time for these conversations and encourage open reflection, they're saying, *"Your energy matters. Your 'why' matters."*

Even more powerful? When leaders model this themselves. Share your own *passions* with your staff. Talk about how your *love for storytelling* influences the way you lead assemblies, or how your *passion for diversity* informs hiring and discipline policies. When school leaders lead with openness, make *values* visible, and invite others to do the same, they create a school culture where *passion* isn't just permitted—it's energizing. It spreads, fuels collaboration, and inspires creativity in unexpected ways. So go ahead—be bold about what drives you. Encourage your team to do the same. Because a school full of passionate educators, aligned in purpose and supported in their growth, is more than a workplace. It's a *community with momentum*.

Below are a few examples of how a principal's *passions* can influence and clarify their decisions and *purpose*:

- **Passion** for *creativity and curiosity* lead to designing environments where every child's unique interests and needs are honored.

- A *love for mentorship* influences how a principal builds leadership capacity within teachers and staff, offering autonomy and growth opportunities.
- *Passion* for *community and belonging* inspires practices that create inclusive, supportive environments that reflect shared *values* and traditions.
- A *passion* for *literacy, STEM, or the arts* may guide strategic investments in curriculum, partnerships, and enrichment programs.
- *Passion* for *human connection* informs how the principal leads with understanding, builds trust, and makes time for meaningful conversations.
- *Passion* for *creativity* drives the principal to find fresh solutions to challenges, embrace risk, and encourage experimentation across the school.
- A deep commitment to *justice* motivates decisions that remove barriers for marginalized students and ensure all voices are heard.
- *Passion* sustains the principal's energy through difficult seasons, serving as a *North Star* when faced with competing priorities.

Are you a teacher? Then you already wear 17 different hats a day—*educator, counselor, cheerleader, nurse, and occasional tech support.* So why not add one more? *Passions Coach.* Help your students uncover what makes them tick (besides lunch and early dismissal) by using these thoughtfully designed lesson plans (Appendix D). Each activity invites students to dig into their interests, explore their weird and wonderful *passions*, and maybe even answer the age-old question: *"What inspires you?"* These lessons aren't just about finding hobbies—they're about helping students connect what they love with what they can do in the world. When students feel like their *passions* matter, school gets a whole lot more meaningful (and a lot less *"why are we learning this?"*). So, dive in, and get ready to help

Classroom Lessons

your students discover what lights them up. You might just find yourself inspired along the way, too.

In the end, *passion* is not just a spark—it's the *fire that lights the way* toward a life of *purpose*. When we align what we do with what we love and what we believe, we unlock a version of ourselves that is *vibrant, resilient*, and *deeply impactful*. For educators, this isn't just about lesson plans or test scores—it's about *leading with heart, teaching with joy*, and *showing up with integrity* even on the hardest days. *Passion* makes learning contagious, relationships transformative, and classrooms places of magic. So, whether you're *choreographing grammar lesson musicals, making frog dissections look fun*, or simply showing up every day with your sleeves rolled and heart open, know this:

Your *passion* matters.

Your *values* matter.

And when you lead with both, you don't just teach—you *inspire*.

Let your *values* be your compass, your *passion* be your fuel, and your *purpose* be your legacy.

Passions Development Checklist for All School Personnel

Use this checklist to reflect on how you help ignite, support, and sustain passion in your school community. Check all that apply.

<u>Fostering Passion in Myself</u>

- I regularly reflect on what excites and energizes me professionally and personally.
- I carve out time for the aspects of my role I'm most passionate about.
- I look for ways to connect my personal interests to my professional work.
- I talk about my passions with students and colleagues to model authentic engagement.

Encouraging Passion in Students

- I create opportunities for students to explore their interests in meaningful ways.
- I notice what lights students up and provide space for those passions to grow.
- I connect classroom learning to real-world topics that students care about.
- I offer choices in how students express learning, allowing room for creativity and curiosity.

Supporting Passion Among Colleagues

- I show interest in my colleagues' passions—inside and outside of education.
- I encourage team members to bring their strengths and interests into collaborative projects.
- I celebrate colleagues who go above and beyond because they love what they do.
- I advocate for roles, projects, or professional development that align with my team's passions.

Creating a Culture Where Passion Thrives

- I contribute to a school culture where enthusiasm, innovation, and creativity are valued.
- I support initiatives that encourage people to try new things—even if they fail.
- I recognize and honor small moments of passion-driven excellence (e.g., hallway displays, student clubs, creative lessons).
- I help create safe, inclusive spaces where everyone feels encouraged to explore what matters to them.

Vision from the Field

Kiesha: As an instructional coach, my passion for helping others realize their potential is at the heart of my purpose. I believe that when teachers feel supported, valued, and inspired, that energy ripples directly into their classrooms and ultimately benefits every student. I'm passionate about collaboration, and that shapes the way I approach coaching—not as an evaluator, but as a thought partner, a listener, and a fellow learner. I find joy in seeing teachers grow in confidence, try something new, and reflect with pride on the impact they're making. That passion drives me to be present, curious, and intentional in every conversation, because I know that when teachers thrive, students do too.

Hana: As an assistant principal, my passion for creating safe, inclusive spaces where every student feels a sense of belonging is what fuels my leadership. I'm driven by the belief that relationships come first—before instruction, before discipline, before anything else. That belief shapes how I approach each day: whether I'm supporting a student through a tough moment, partnering with a teacher to navigate a classroom challenge, or helping design systems that promote belonging. I am especially passionate about developing people. I find deep purpose in helping staff grow through coaching, honest feedback, and celebrating their strengths. I lead with honesty and consistency because I want both students and adults to know they can count on me. That trust creates the foundation for everything else. My role isn't just about managing behavior or enforcing rules; it's about modeling the culture we want to build. My passion for leadership, justice, and growth keeps me grounded and reminds me that every interaction is a chance to inspire, uplift, and move the school closer to its vision.

Challenge: Add your Voice on Passions.

Email us at Purposestories@quagliainstitute.org and upload your story. Feel free to identify yourself and your school (or remain anonymous).

References

J.M. Jachimowicz, A. Wihler, E.R. Bailey, & A.D. Galinsky, Why grit requires perseverance and passion to positively predict performance, *Proc. Natl. Acad. Sci. U.S.A.* 115 (40) 9980-9985, https://doi.org/10.1073/pnas.1803561115 (2018).

Frenzel, A. C., Goetz, T., Lüdtke, O., Pekrun, R., & Sutton, R. E. (2009). *Emotional transmission in the classroom: Exploring the relationship between teacher and student enjoyment.* Journal of Educational Psychology, 101(3), 705–716.

Pianta, R. C., Hamre, B. K., & Allen, J. P. (2012). *Teacher-student relationships and engagement: Conceptualizing, measuring, and improving the capacity of classroom interactions.* In Christenson, Reschly, & Wylie (Eds.), *Handbook of Research on Student Engagement* (pp. 365–386). Springer.

Poulou, M. S. (2017). Students' emotional and behavioral difficulties: the role of teachers' social and emotional learning and teacher-student relationships. International Journal of Emotional Education,9, 72-89, Retrieved April 11, 2022, from https://files.eric.ed.gov/fulltext/EJ1197559.pdf.

Roorda, D. L., Koomen, H. M., Spilt, J. L., & Oort, F. J. (2011). *The influence of affective teacher–student relationships on students' school engagement and achievement: A meta-analytic approach.* Review of Educational Research, 81(4), 493–529.

Ryan, R. M., & Deci, E. L. (2000). *Intrinsic and extrinsic motivations: Classic definitions and new directions.* Contemporary Educational Psychology, 25(1), 54–67.

04 | Vision and Voyage:

The Interplay of Aspirations and Purpose

*The future belongs to those who believe
in the beauty of their dreams.*

– Eleanor Roosevelt

> Aspirations represent an individual's hopes and dreams for the future while being inspired in the present to reach those dreams. When educators work toward their hopes, they are driven by a vision of what they wish to achieve or become. Pursuing and achieving one's aspirations can validate personal capabilities and significantly enhance an educator's sense of purpose.

While passions fuel our present with energy and excitement, aspirations take that momentum and shape it into a vision for the future, transforming what we love to do into who we strive to become. Think back for a moment—*what did you dream about when you were a kid?* Maybe you wanted to be a firefighter, a singer, a veterinarian, or the first person to live on Mars. Maybe you dreamed of writing a book, building a treehouse, or just having a best friend who really got you. For some of us, those memories might be blurry—faded snapshots tucked deep into childhood. But no matter our age or stage in life, we all carry with us hopes and dreams. They shift and evolve as we grow.

An elementary school student may dream of finally being able to read chapter books like their older sibling. A middle schooler might hope to find where they belong, to feel accepted. A high school student may quietly wonder what's next—college, a job, the unknown. And the reality is that some days, a teacher simply dreams of making it to their lunch break with their sanity intact.

But here's the thing: *did your childhood dreams come true?* Or did they fade away like so many New Year's resolutions—boldly declared, briefly pursued, then quietly forgotten when no fairy godmother appeared to make the dream come to life?

Dreams are beautiful. They give us direction. They give us *purpose*. They help us imagine a better future and visualize what could be. But here's the hard truth—*dreams without action are just a dime a dozen*. Take the student who dreams of learning to read. That dream doesn't come true by accident. It comes from trying, failing, sounding out words, and reading every day—even when it's hard. It comes from encouragement, perseverance, and practice. The same goes for the adult who sets a resolution to run a 5K, save more money, or eat healthier. Without effort—without lacing up the shoes, making a budget, or skipping that midnight snack—nothing changes. Dreams need a partner, and that partner is *aspiration*.

Aspirations turn dreams into action. They are dreams with a backbone. They're the commitment to not just dream of something but to *work* for it. *Aspirations* require a plan, daily choices, and a mindset that believes *"I can do this"*—even on days when the finish line feels far away. So the question isn't just *"What do you dream about?"* It's also: *"What are you doing to make that dream come true?"* Because when you combine *passion* with persistence, and dreams with determination, amazing things can happen. *Aspirations* represent an individual's hopes and dreams for the future while being inspired in the present to reach those dreams. When educators work toward their hopes, they are driven by a vision of what they want to achieve or become. Pursuing and achieving one's *aspirations* can validate personal capabilities and significantly enhance an educator's sense of *purpose*.

Aspirations are the heart and soul of an educator's journey—equal parts dreaming and doing. They're not just whimsical musings whispered over a snack in the staff lounge; they are grounded visions of what an educator seeks to accomplish or become. Whether it's igniting a lifelong love of music in every student, revolutionizing outdated curriculum, or becoming the principal who finally fixes the broken copier *and* the school culture, *aspirations* provide both *purpose* and fuel. Each goal stems from a desire to make a significant impact. This vision provides continuous inspiration and serves as a catalyst to one's *purpose*, keeping educators motivated even amidst the everyday challenges of the classroom.

Educators who set their sights on specific *aspirations* dedicate themselves to a path of personal and professional growth. The pursuit of these goals involves more than the day-to-day tasks of teaching; it includes ongoing education, professional development, and sometimes, advocacy. As they work toward these *aspirations*, educators develop new competencies and expand their skill sets. Each step forward is a step toward becoming the educator they aspire to be, which in turn, instills a greater sense of self-efficacy and fulfillment in their roles.

Educators who actively chase their dreams engage in constant growth—attending PD workshops, reflecting on their practice, staying up late adjusting lesson plans, or even writing grant proposals in their pajamas to fund a class greenhouse. Each action builds new skills and a deeper belief in their ability to lead change, no matter how small or large. And when those dreams start to come true—whether it's seeing students thrive, implementing a new mental health initiative, or being nominated for *Teacher of the Year*—it's more than just success. It's *validation* that their work matters.

A teacher striving for an inclusive classroom might pursue training in differentiated instruction or earn certification in special education. An aspiring school leader may begin mentoring colleagues, serve on leadership committees, or enroll in an advanced degree program. These are more than professional goals—they're expressions of a deeper "why": a desire to make a difference that reaches beyond classroom walls.

And let's be honest—education isn't for the faint of heart. Some days, the Wi-Fi's down, it's pizza day in the cafeteria, and you realize you've been passionately lecturing to a room full of glazed-over eyes. On days like that, it's not checklists that keep educators going—it's the vision. Aspirations act like lighthouses, reminding educators that the chaos of today is part of a meaningful journey toward tomorrow.

Over time, that pursuit shapes more than outcomes—it shapes identity. Suddenly, grading isn't about percentages; it's about growth. Morning meetings aren't just routine—they're relational. Hallway hellos become touchpoints of connection. Everything gains depth and purpose. Aspirations mold how educators teach, lead, and love what they do. Even the wildest dreams—whether it's transforming school culture or building a rooftop garden—don't just change the dreamer. They uplift the entire school community.

Driven to Make a Difference: The Role of Aspirations in Educational Success

Aspirations begin with permission to dream. And in a profession as demanding as education, that permission matters. Educators need space to imagine what *could be*—to picture a classroom where multilingual students proudly share their stories, a library buzzing with community engagement, or a school that shapes national policy instead of just reacting to it.

Picture a science teacher who envisions an outdoor lab for ecosystem exploration. Or a counselor who dreams of launching an alumni mentorship network to build generational support. These aren't fantasies—they're seedlings of purpose. When educators reflect on what excites them, they begin to uncover the dreams worth pursuing.

But dreams don't become reality without direction. Aspirations require action. That means translating vision into clear, future-focused goals. A teacher might pursue National Board Certification to deepen their impact. A leader might develop a culturally responsive curriculum that celebrates every student's identity. These goals, grounded in values and passion, are more than achievable—they're sustaining. They anchor the dream in purpose.

Daily moments provide fuel along the way. A middle school teacher watches a once-hesitant reader devour a novel. A music teacher hears a shy student shine during a solo. These aren't just milestones. They're reminders that every effort ripples outward. They transform the mundane into meaningful and keep the bigger vision in focus.

Aspirations flourish in a mindset of lifelong learning, not just for students, but for teachers, too. When educators stay curious, they stay vital. An elementary teacher might learn coding and launch a robotics club. A school leader might finally submit the article they've been mentally writing for years. A willingness to evolve keeps aspirations alive—and makes them resilient in the face of setbacks because a growth mindset reframes failure as feedback and struggle as the soil of success.

Surrounding yourself with a community of dreamers makes the journey richer. Collaborating with mentors, peers, or professional networks offers accountability, encouragement, and a fresh perspective. Think of a team of teachers who co-author a grant for an artist-in-residence program. Or educators who start a podcast to share their stories. Shared aspiration multiplies momentum—and often uncovers opportunities one person alone might miss.

Hopes and Dreams: The Power Behind the Promise

Hopes and dreams are powerful. They give us purpose. They offer something to look forward to—something larger than our current reality. For many of us, dreaming comes naturally—sometimes so naturally that it feels automatic, even mindless. We dream while zoning out in class, staring out the window, or drifting off to sleep.

Video

But dreaming is only the beginning.

Here's the catch: without action, a dream is just a wish dressed up in fancy words. And *aspiration*—that beautiful word we see on motivational posters and hear in graduation speeches—can quickly become hollow if it's not backed by effort.

Think about the dreams we often hear from students:
- "I want to be a doctor."
- "I want to be a marine biologist."
- "I want to be a carpenter."
- "I want to be in the police force."

These are bold, exciting dreams—and they should be celebrated. But then we hear the next part:
- "I want to be a doctor, but I failed biology."
- "I want to be a marine biologist, but I don't want to go in the ocean."
- "I want to be a carpenter, but I don't like math."
- "I want to be a police officer, but I don't like following rules."

Suddenly, those dreams feel a little... complicated.

Now, this doesn't mean the dreams are impossible. It just means they require work. *Real, consistent,* sometimes *uncomfortable* work. That's the difference between hoping and aspiring. A *hope* is something we want. An *aspiration* is something we're willing to pursue.

That's where the *Aspirations Profile* comes in. It offers a meaningful framework to better understand what drives us—and what holds us back. It helps students (and adults) identify not only what they want to become, but also what they're doing right now to get there. It highlights the power of *belief, motivation,* and *engagement*.

Because at the end of the day, dreaming big is essential. But *doing the work*—that's what transforms a dream into a destination.

So yes, let's keep encouraging students and educators to dream. Let them imagine careers, futures, adventures. But let's also help them connect those dreams to today's choices—one step, one action, one chapter of biology at a time.

Aspirations Profile

	Low — Doing — High
High Dreaming — **Imagination**: Sets goals for the future, but does not put forth the effort to reach those goals.	**Aspiration**: Sets goals for the future, and puts forth effort in the present to reach those goals.
Hibernation: Has no goals for the future, and puts in no effort in the present.	**Perspiration**: Works hard in the present, but has no goals for the future.

Hibernation

Someone in *Hibernation* doesn't think much about the future, has no clear goals, and puts forth minimal effort in daily life. Educators in this quadrant have lost the passion that once drove them to teach and to transform lives. At best, they appear complacent; at worst, they're disengaged entirely. These teachers often operate in isolation, spending most of their time alone in their classrooms, disconnected from colleagues and the broader school community. They feel stuck. Lesson planning is uninspired, instructional delivery lacks energy, and each school day drags on—both for them and their students.

For these educators, the classroom becomes a place of routine rather than purpose. Instruction feels dull to the teacher, let alone to the students. Others may describe them as "checked out," simply waiting for the next summer break or retirement. Whether labeled as burnt out, unmotivated, or just going through the motions, what they're truly missing is a sense of meaning and momentum.

- When do you notice yourself slipping into *Hibernation*?
- What is happening around you—and within you—during those times?

Perspiration

Someone in *Perspiration* works extremely hard but lacks a clear direction. These educators are known for their strong work ethic and unwavering dedication. They show up early, stay late, serve on multiple committees, and take on task after task. Yet despite all their effort, they often feel like they're running in place. There is little forward movement, either in their teaching practices or in student learning outcomes.

Teachers in this quadrant may appear driven on the outside, but underneath, there's a growing sense of frustration. The return on their investment—emotionally, professionally, and academically—feels low. Their calendars are full, but their sense of progress is empty. Over time, this imbalance can lead to exhaustion and burnout.

- What are some things you work incredibly hard at but find little satisfaction in?
- What would it take for your hard work to feel genuinely meaningful and rewarding?

Imagination

Someone in *Imagination* readily shares their hopes and dreams, yet struggles to act on them. Teachers in this quadrant overflow with positivity and creative ideas. They are often the first to champion a new program, eagerly contribute to visioning sessions, and speak passionately about students, school culture, and educational innovation. They are optimistic, encouraging, and often seen as the "spark" in conversations about school improvement.

But when it comes to translating ideas into action, they fall short. Follow-through is inconsistent or absent. Their intentions are admirable, but their outcomes are few. As a result, they may be perceived as unrealistic, overly idealistic, or even disingenuous—described as having their head in the clouds, full of enthusiasm but light on execution.

- What are your biggest hopes and dreams for your classroom, school, or career?
- What tangible steps can you begin taking to move from dreaming to doing?

Aspiration

Someone in *Aspiration* not only dreams of a better future but actively works to achieve it. These educators are grounded in vision and committed to action. They set meaningful goals—both short-term and long-term—and consistently take steps toward them. They are dependable, energetic, and resourceful. Their ability to *dream and do* makes them invaluable contributors to the school community.

Teachers in this quadrant don't fear failure—they learn from it. They embrace innovation, seek feedback, and maintain a steady focus on growth. They show up fully, day after day, not only for their students but for their colleagues and their school. Their participation in professional conversations is thoughtful, honest, and constructive. They uplift the culture through both words and actions.

These teachers understand their job is more than a role—it's a privilege. They are committed to continuous improvement not only in their classrooms but across the school, because they believe every student deserves the best version of education possible.

- What goals are you currently working towards achieving?
- Reflect on a goal you recently accomplished and what it took to reach that goal.

Of course, the *Aspirations Profile* isn't just for teachers, though let's be honest, they're often the overachieving type who color-code their dreams. Whether you're in the classroom, coaching from the sidelines, leading a school or district, or still a student trying to figure out what you want to be when you grow up (no pressure—you've got your whole life), the core idea stays the same: **dreaming and doing matter.**

Understanding the power of having big dreams—and actually taking steps to pursue them—is essential for building a lasting sense of purpose. It's not about having all the answers. It's about having the courage to ask the right questions and then take that awkward, exhilarating, possibly wearing two different socks first step forward.

Purpose doesn't show up in a fancy envelope or with a dramatic soundtrack (though wouldn't that be amazing?). It's built, moment by moment—in classrooms, in boardrooms, in hallway chats, and during late-night lesson planning marathons. The *Aspirations Profile* reminds us that it's okay to dream big, stumble along the way, and keep going. Because that's how purpose takes root, grows, and ultimately makes a real impact.

If we can help students—and adults—believe that their voices matter and their dreams are worth chasing… well, that's kind of magical, isn't it?

Why Aspirations Matter: More Than Just a Buzzword

Supporting student aspirations isn't a passing educational trend—it's foundational to helping them reach their full potential. Aspirations go beyond casual daydreams. They are *future-focused goals* that shape behavior, influence decision-making, and drive perseverance, especially when challenges arise.

A compelling study in the *European Economic Review* (2022) confirmed that student aspirations significantly impact long-term educational and career outcomes, even after accounting for socioeconomic background and cognitive ability (Attanasio et al., 2022). In other words, simply believing in a meaningful, attainable future can be a powerful game-changer, particularly for students from disadvantaged or underrepresented backgrounds.

Other research echoes this. Gutman and Akerman (2008), in a report for the Institute of Education, found that high aspirations correlate with greater academic achievement and resilience. The *ASPIRE Programme* in the UK (Strand & Winston, 2008) showed that structured aspiration-building initiatives reduce achievement gaps and fuel student motivation.

But aspirations don't flourish in a vacuum. They require validation, structure, and a shared belief that dreams are worth working for. Students need schools, teachers, mentors, and families who not only encourage their goals but help them understand how to pursue them with clarity, commitment, and confidence.

Quaglia and Corso (2014) underscored this in *Student Voice: The Instrument of Change*, emphasizing that when students feel heard and believe their dreams matter, engagement and achievement rise. Supporting student aspirations isn't just best practice—it's a strategy for equity, empowerment, and lasting success.

Discussion: Agree or Disagree?
- Encouraging all of the students' dreams isn't realistic. Agree? Disagree?
- It's easy for students to dream; the challenge is the doing. Agree? Disagree?
- Aspirations matter most for high school students. Agree? Disagree?
- Teachers' aspirations should align with their school's mission. Agree? Disagree?

Igniting the Inner Flame: Aspirations Fueled by Values and Passion

Aspirations live in the space between dreaming and doing. They're bold, personal declarations of what matters most. When grounded in values, they transcend ambition and become a reflection of identity: *This* is who I am. This is what I stand for. This is what I'm chasing—with heart, hustle, and maybe a little chocolate.

Think of the teacher who dreams of transforming a dusty school library into a vibrant, inclusive writing hub because they believe every child deserves to see themselves in a book. Or the school administrator so committed to food equity that they spend weekends digging through grant databases to fund free meals and pantry access. These aren't tasks. They're *purpose projects*.

And what fuels them? Passion.

Passion is the jet fuel of aspiration. It's the thing that keeps you revising a lesson plan at midnight because you know it could be better. It's why a fifth-grade teacher might sing "Fraction Funk" mid-math class just to light up a student's face (true story—it was a hit). Passion gives us grit, creativity, and the absurdly optimistic belief that we can change lives—even during indoor recess after a snow day.

Aspirations powered by values and passion don't just move us forward—they keep us going when things get hard. And they remind us why we started in the first place.

And here's the fun part: when your *values*, *passions*, and *aspirations* align, something special happens. You know the feeling. The lesson flopped, your inbox looks like a crime scene, and—of course—the air conditioner broke ten minutes before open house. Still, something inside you holds steady. That quiet inner voice reminds you that *you're in this because you believe in growth, creativity, and making your corner of the world a little better.*

That clarity? It keeps the fire burning when the winds of change, doubt, or bureaucracy blow hard. It turns everyday setbacks into opportunities for deeper meaning. The teacher who values *perseverance* sees a struggling student not as a failure, but as a call to dig deeper. The counselor who prioritizes *student voice* doesn't burn out from difficult conversations—instead, they're energized by the privilege of making someone feel seen.

Ultimately, the most fulfilling goals are those that don't just take us somewhere—they *transform* us along the way. When our aspirations are rooted in what we believe and fueled by what we love, our lives become more than a checklist of tasks or trophies. They become a story. A living narrative of growth, purpose, and impact.

So go ahead. Dream big. Set bold, beautiful goals. Start that after-school garden club. Apply for that leadership role. Write the curriculum that makes students light up with curiosity. Because when your aspirations are powered by values and passion, you're not just hitting milestones—you're lighting the way for others to follow.

Vision and Voyage: Next Steps

Activity

Are you a school leader? If so, you have more than a role—you have a responsibility and a rare opportunity. You can shape not just instruction and logistics, but the *culture* that surrounds and supports your team. Fostering teacher aspirations isn't just a thoughtful gesture. It's a strategic investment in morale, retention, and student achievement.

When educators are given the space to reflect on their future dreams, they become more focused and inspired in the present. Their aspirations shape how they approach their students, structure their lessons, and build relationships with their peers. Teachers who feel seen, heard, and supported are far more likely to pass that care and intention on to their classrooms.

One way to make this reflection real is by using the Aspirations Audit (see Appendix E). This simple tool helps educators clarify their values, set meaningful goals, and better understand how their aspirations influence their work. What begins as personal growth quickly evolves into schoolwide momentum. Purpose becomes contagious.

Make it a priority to carve out intentional space for these reflections during staff meetings, professional development days, or informal check-ins. When leaders model sincerity, live their values out loud, and invite others to do the same, they don't just *allow* aspirations—they *ignite* them. They build a school culture where dreaming big isn't a side note—it's the headline.

In environments like these, aspirations don't just survive. They *thrive*. They're nurtured, celebrated, and shared. And when that happens, everyone rises.

As a leader, consider how you implement and support the following practices that support aspirations. School Leaders can:

1. Foster a Culture of Growth

- Initiate regular one-on-one meetings to discuss career goals and growth opportunities.
- Encourage goal setting as part of yearly evaluations—not just for performance, but for aspirations.
- Celebrate milestones (certifications earned, advanced degrees, leadership roles taken).
- Model aspirational behavior by sharing your own goals and professional journey.

2. Provide Professional Development Opportunities

- Offer differentiated PD options based on individual teacher interests and goals.
- Support conference attendance and provide funding or coverage when possible.
- Promote action research or innovation grants within the school or district.
- Invite guest speakers or mentors from outside fields to broaden exposure.

3. Create Leadership Pathways

- Empower teachers to lead committees, professional learning communities, or special projects.
- Identify and cultivate teacher leaders for instructional coaching, mentoring, or department chairs.
- Provide "stretch assignments" (e.g., leading PD, school initiatives) aligned with teacher interests.
- Advocate for aspiring leaders when district-level opportunities arise.

4. Personalize Support and Encouragement

- Ask about aspirations—not just professionally, but personally. Show genuine interest.
- Write recommendation letters, endorse on LinkedIn, or nominate for awards.
- Help set SMART goals and check in periodically on progress.
- Celebrate risk-taking and allow space for failure as part of the growth process.

5. Remove Barriers to Aspiration

- Streamline administrative tasks so teachers can focus on teaching and growth.
- Create a psychologically safe environment where innovation and ambition are supported.
- Provide coverage or flexibility for teachers pursuing graduate courses or certifications.
- Advocate for equitable access to advancement opportunities for all staff.

6. Cultivate a Vision-Driven Community

- Connect aspirations to the school's mission and long-term vision.
- Encourage collaboration across grade levels and departments to share strengths and talents.
- Host "aspiration forums" or career mapping sessions to build collective energy and inspiration.
- Include teacher voice in school decisions to promote ownership and professional agency.

Classroom Lessons

Are you a teacher? Then we invite you to bring these classroom lessons to life and help your students explore their *aspirations* in meaningful, imaginative ways. These activities (see Appendix F) are designed to spark conversations about dreaming big and actually doing something about it. Because while "professional video gamer" may not be the dream you pictured, it *is* a conversation starter. And that's where the magic begins.

These lessons give students a way to explore what excites them, what drives them, and how to connect their passions to real-world possibilities. Think of it as handing them a flashlight and a map—not just saying, "*Good luck, figure it out.*"

So dive in. Ask the big questions. Encourage the wild ideas. Laugh when someone says they want to be a dinosaur when they grow up (hey, that's creativity at work). Because when we make space for *both* dreaming and doing, we're not just preparing kids for the future—we're giving them the confidence and clarity to *shape* it.

Aspirations as a Calling

In the end, aspirations are more than career goals or tasks on a to-do list. They're reflections of who we are and what we value. They're born of *passion*, sustained by *persistence*, and guided by a deep sense of *purpose*.

For many educators, aspirations begin with something simple: a desire to make a difference. But when that desire is fueled by love for students, belief in equity, and a relentless curiosity for what could be, it becomes something more. It becomes a *calling*.

Whether your dream is to revolutionize reading instruction, start an after-school robotics team, or just make it through one Monday without a technical glitch, keep dreaming. And more importantly, *keep doing*.

Because when passion aligns with purpose, and values light the path forward, there's no limit to the kind of impact an educator can make.

And let's face it—if anyone can turn chaos into clarity, and purpose into change, it's probably *you*. Dry-erase marker in one hand. Twenty-five brilliant, unpredictable, extraordinary minds in the other.

Voices from the Field

Oliver: As a school board member in a rural district, my aspirations are grounded in a deep commitment to ensuring our students have the same opportunities and support as those in any community, regardless of our size or resources. I grew up in a town like this, where schools are more than just buildings—they're the heart of the community. That sense of responsibility drives every decision I make. I aspire to preserve the close-knit values that define rural education—strong relationships, community pride, and personalized learning—while also pushing us to innovate and adapt so our students are prepared for an ever-changing world. Whether it's improving access to technology, expanding career and technical education, or finding creative ways to recruit and retain quality teachers, I want to be part of the solution that brings progress without losing our identity.

These aspirations give purpose to my service. They remind me that my role is not just about governance or policy—it's about shaping a vision for the future of our community. They push me to advocate for funding to support necessary programs, to invest in programs that keep our students competitive, and to listen to every voice, especially those that are often left out. I also see my role as a listener and a connector—someone who bridges the gap between the school and the broader community. My purpose is to ensure that every decision we make keeps students at the center, supports our educators, and strengthens the community as a whole. Ultimately, my aspirations define not just what I hope to achieve, but why I serve: to help create a school system that reflects our rural values, honors our history, and prepares every student for a successful future, whether they stay here or take their talents beyond our town.

Mia. As a middle school track coach, my aspirations go far beyond winning meets or setting records. I aspire to help young athletes discover what they're capable of—physically, mentally, and emotionally. I want each student to walk away from the season not just faster or stronger, but more confident in themselves and more connected to their team. These aspirations shape my purpose every day. I see coaching as a platform to teach life lessons—about perseverance, accountability, and integrity. Track and field offer a unique space where individual effort and team spirit go hand in hand, and I use that dynamic to help students understand the value of personal growth and collective responsibility.

I aspire to build a team culture where every athlete feels seen and valued, regardless of skill level. For some, this is their first time being part of something bigger than themselves. For others, it's a chance to channel energy into something positive. Either way, I know that how I show up—as a mentor, motivator, and role model—directly influences how they see themselves. My purpose is to create more than athletes—I want to help shape young people who are respectful, determined, and unafraid to push themselves past what they thought was possible. My aspirations keep me grounded in that mission. Whether we're practicing starts, running relays, or reflecting after a tough meet, I know I'm not just coaching for the season—I'm coaching for their future.

Challenge: Add your Voice on Aspirations. Email us at Purposestories@quagliainstitute.org and upload your story. Feel free to identify yourself and your school (or remain anonymous).

Aspirations Development Checklist for All School Personnel

Use this checklist to reflect on how well you support the development of aspirations in yourself, your students, and your colleagues. Check all that apply.

Supporting Aspirations in Myself

- I take time to reflect on my own dreams, goals, and what I hope to accomplish in my career.
- I create intentional steps toward my long-term aspirations—even if they're small.
- I stay connected to my "why" and use it to stay focused through challenges.
- I acknowledge when I'm evolving and adjust my goals accordingly.
- I celebrate progress toward my dreams, not just the big wins.

Nurturing Aspirations in Students

- I provide space for students to talk about their hopes, goals, and dreams—no matter how big or small.
- I connect classroom content to real-life goals and future possibilities.
- I reinforce the idea that effort, persistence, and planning are essential for achieving dreams.
- I help students understand that failure is part of the path to success.
- I offer encouragement and specific feedback that builds students' belief in themselves.

Empowering Aspirations Among Colleagues

- I engage in meaningful conversations with colleagues about their professional goals and aspirations.
- I offer support, collaboration, or mentorship to help others pursue their aspirations.

- I celebrate others' growth, transitions, and accomplishments.
- I advocate for professional learning and leadership opportunities aligned with individual passions and goals.
- I help foster a workplace culture where dreams are taken seriously and pursued.

Creating an Aspirations-Focused Culture
- I believe every educator and student has a unique purpose and potential.
- I promote long-term thinking by encouraging vision boards, goal-setting, or "future self" reflections.
- I talk about dreaming *and* doing, not just inspiration, but action steps.
- I recognize the link between passion and aspiration and help others make that connection.
- I contribute to a school climate that treats aspirations as more than energy—as fuel for purpose, perseverance, and impact.

References

Attanasio, O., Cattan, S., Fitzsimons, E., Meghir, C., & Rubio-Codina, M. (2022). Aspirations and educational investment: Evidence from an experiment in Colombia. *European Economic Review, 145,* 104114.

Gutman, L. M., & Akerman, R. (2008). *Determinants of aspirations.* Institute of Education, University of London.

Quaglia, R. J., & Corso, M. J. (2014). *Student voice: The instrument of change.* Corwin Press.

Strand, S., & Winston, J. (2008). *Educational aspirations in inner city schools.* University of Warwick.

Lekfuangfu, W. N., & Odermatt, R. (2022). All I have to do is dream? The role of aspirations in intergenerational mobility and well-being. *European Economic Review, 148.*

05 | Purpose in Practice:

Cultivating Your Talents

The meaning of life is to find your gift.
The purpose of life is to give it away.
— **Pablo Picasso**

> Talents are the interplay between a person's natural gifts, acquired skills, and lived experiences. This combination of innate strengths, learned abilities, and meaningful interactions with the world helps individuals lead more purpose-driven and satisfying lives. For educators, understanding and embracing their talents contributes to both personal growth and professional success. It also enhances their ability to meaningfully connect and engage with students and colleagues.

While *aspirations* give us a vision of who we want to become, it's our *talents*—those often-overlooked strengths and instincts—that quietly prepare us for the journey. Before we can fully chase our dreams, we must first recognize the unique tools we already carry—the ones that feel effortless when we're in our element.

Have you ever noticed how some things just *click* for you? Maybe you can explain complex ideas with ease. Or maybe you're the calming presence when chaos erupts in the classroom. These moments often go unnoticed—not because they're insignificant, but because they feel so natural. And that's exactly where your talents hide: not in spotlight moments, but in the subtleties of how you work, connect, and lead.

Talents aren't always loud. They don't demand applause. In fact, they're often disguised as *"just how I do things."* But here's the secret: when we pause long enough to name those patterns—those instinctive actions, reactions, and skills—we begin to unlock a powerful toolkit that can shape how we live, learn, and lead.

Talents Are Seeds, Not Statues

Think of talents as seeds of greatness. Some you're born with. Others you collect and cultivate over time. But whether natural or nurtured, they're bursting with possibility.

Still, *potential isn't enough.* Talents need sunlight (*reflection*), water (*practice*), and a little weeding (*growth mindset*) to truly thrive. So, the better question isn't just *what* your talents are, but *what could they become* if you gave them room to grow?

Now imagine bringing that discovery process into your classroom, your team meetings, or your own personal development. *What would change if we treated our talents not as accidents, but as intentional parts of our purpose?*

Research in positive education supports this shift. Studies show that encouraging students to recognize and use their strengths leads to greater engagement, motivation, and well-being (Seligman et al., 2009). What you do with ease—what comes naturally to you, while others struggle—often holds the key to your hidden strengths. Talents aren't just things you get praised for. They're the subtle, instinctive actions that quietly shape how you show up in the world.

And when those talents are acknowledged, nurtured, and directed with purpose? They become more than personality traits. They become *tools* for purpose, fulfillment, and impact.

What's Your Talent Hiding As?

We often think of talents as fixed traits—"She's the math whiz," or "He's the creative one." But real talent? It's far more layered than that.

It's a mix of natural gifts, learned skills, and lived experiences—stirred together to create the unique recipe of *you*. Your talent for storytelling may have started with childhood bedtime tales, sharpened through years of writing, and been supercharged the day you led a school-wide assembly without fainting. That's talent in motion.

Real talent is dynamic. It grows. It adapts. It evolves. The most effective educators don't just *have* talent—they *invest in it*. They reflect. They practice. They stretch themselves. They turn sparks into steady flames.

Walk into any school and you'll see talent alive and well. A teacher who quiets a stormy classroom with a single glance. A counselor who knows exactly what to say and when. A music teacher who gets 30 middle schoolers to sing in harmony—and *enjoy* it.

Teachers as Talent Architects

Educators are not only carriers of talent—they're *architects* of it. Their role isn't just to recognize their strengths, but to cultivate them with intention. In doing so, they model what it looks like to live a purpose-driven, growth-minded professional life.

Talents are formed where natural gifts, acquired skills, and real-life experience intersect. And when educators engage with their talents over time, they uncover deeper gifts and develop broader capacities, expanding their impact in the process.

Research continues to highlight the connection between strengths-based approaches and positive youth development. Knowing and using one's talents has been shown to boost well-being, self-esteem, and life satisfaction in both children and adolescents (Waters, 2014a, 2014b; Allan & Duffy, 2014; Douglass & Duffy, 2015).

In schools, this is visible every day. It's there in the confidence of a teacher trying something new. In the steady hand of a leader, navigating uncertainty. In the patience of a mentor who sees possibility where others might see limits.

- A teacher may have a natural ability to sense students' moods and emotional cues. But it's through professional learning—such as trauma-informed training, restorative practices, and years of building trusting relationships—that this strength grows into a powerful tool for student connection and classroom culture. Over time, their room becomes a safe haven where students feel seen, supported, and empowered to take academic and emotional risks.
- A kindergarten teacher with a natural sense of rhythm incorporates music into transitions and routines, turning chaos into choreography.
- A chemistry teacher who struggled in school shares that story with students, building trust and showing that struggle is part of success.
- A school counselor blends active listening with trauma-informed training, helping students feel seen, heard, and supported—even on their hardest days.

Natural gifts—like an ear for music, a mind for numbers, or the ability to command a room—often serve as the starting blocks of our journey. These innate strengths shape early interests and steer initial efforts. A natural listener may gravitate toward counseling or teaching. A born storyteller might find their rhythm in writing or leadership. When these gifts align with personal *values*—like a desire to help others or a passion for equity—they don't just lead to success. They create *meaning*. Daily tasks become more than just duties—they become expressions of purpose.

But gifts alone aren't enough.

Experiences—from life's curveballs to career milestones—shape and sharpen those gifts into something truly impactful. Each challenge, each success, and yes, even each awkward parent-teacher conference, becomes a tool for transformation. Experiences add emotional depth and practical wisdom, helping us use our talents more effectively and adapt them to shifting aspirations.

For educators, this interplay between gifts and experience is where the magic really happens.

Maybe you start with an instinct for calming a room or explaining a tough concept. But it's the day-to-day lived reality—reality-the tough conversations, the curriculum pivots, the missed buses, and the hallway heart-to-hearts—that molds those instincts into enduring strengths. These moments aren't just teaching you *what* you're good at—they're teaching you *when*, *why*, and *how* to use your talents with purpose.

In this way, experiences are both a mirror and a mold: they reflect where you're already strong, and shape who you're becoming.

Building Your Unique Talent Profile

Natural gifts. Learned skills. Lived experiences. Together, they form your *talent profile*—your unique combination of strengths and strategies for navigating life, work, and relationships. This profile becomes your lens for seeing the world and making choices that align with what you truly value.

In education, this is more than just professional self-awareness. It's a roadmap for leadership, service, and growth.

Take, for example, a school counselor whose natural talent is compassion. Pair that with years of guiding students through everything from playground drama to identity crises, and you've got someone who can de-escalate an emotional meltdown before it even starts. They listen between the lines. They ask the right questions. They even know exactly where the emergency granola bars are stashed. Their talent profile enables them to build trust quickly, support difficult decisions, and connect families, students, and teachers with empathy and grace.

Or picture an assistant principal with a knack for systems thinking and a core value of innovation. Years of navigating school improvement plans, parent meetings, and the cryptic logic of state assessments have transformed their instincts into something deeper. They don't just organize—they reimagine. Their talent isn't just in knowing what to do—it's in making others believe it *can* be done, even if it involves spreadsheets, highlighters, and an "I promise this will make sense in five minutes" whiteboard session.

Your talents are the *foundation*. Your skills are the *structure*. And your experiences? They're the slightly unpredictable—but always enlightening—home improvement projects that turn the house into a home.

Talent Takes Intention

Here's the truth: talent doesn't grow on autopilot.

It takes *attention* and *intention*. Just like a plant needs sunlight, water, and a little pruning, your strengths need *practice*, *feedback*, and *time*.

A gifted writer becomes an impactful voice by rewriting, revising, and showing up to the page on both the good days and the hard ones. A naturally engaging teacher becomes a transformative force by experimenting with new methods, learning from failure, and staying open to growth.

Whether it's leading a book study, coaching the soccer team, or organizing a schoolwide kindness campaign, these lived experiences build and deepen talent. They help educators move from *pretty good* to *powerhouse*.

And every time we invest in developing our own talents, we're doing more than improving ourselves. We're modeling something essential for our students: Growth is possible. Potential can be developed. And everyone has something worth cultivating.

Lifelong Learning: The Engine of Talent Expansion

The process of developing one's talents is inseparable from the journey of lifelong learning. When people intentionally invest in their strengths—through education, reflection, and practice—they often uncover deeper layers of ability. That discovery leads not only to greater confidence but to entirely new opportunities.

Take, for example, a naturally gifted speaker. With training and experience, that individual might become a powerful negotiator, a compelling storyteller, or a motivational force in both professional and personal spaces. Talents don't exist in a vacuum—they grow through *intention*. They thrive when paired with practice and purpose.

Video

Consider the teacher who loves writing and enrolls in a summer institute for educators. That same teacher might later launch a student literary magazine, giving young writers a platform—and a voice. Or the coach who leads a weekend service project and ends up mentoring future leaders far beyond the sports field. These experiences don't just build skills. They *build identity*. They reinforce purpose, strengthen community, and point toward new paths for contribution and impact.

When Talent Comes Alive in Schools

In the world of education, well-developed talents don't just make a difference—they often delight us in the most unexpected ways. Educators who lean into their unique strengths can turn a regular school day into a memory that sticks long past graduation.

Like the science teacher who transforms every lab into a comedy sketch (*"Don't worry, it's only mildly flammable"*). Or the history teacher who reenacts battles using plastic figurines, epic music, and just the right amount of overacting. These moments don't just make lessons memorable—they make learning *magnetic*. They make classrooms feel alive. They make students want to show up, not just because they have to, but because something *might happen*—something funny, something moving, something real.

And when students are encouraged to discover and grow *their* talents? Magic happens.

A quiet student who doodles in the margins becomes the go-to illustrator for every group project. The high-energy kid who can't sit still suddenly finds purpose on stage, leading the school play with the confidence of a Broadway headliner—or at least a viral TikTok star in the making.

When talents are recognized and nurtured, students gain more than academic knowledge. They gain *confidence*. They find *direction*. They begin to see their own worth, not just in test scores, but in the value of their contributions.

This kind of talent cultivation doesn't just elevate individuals—it transforms communities. Classrooms become more creative, collaborative, and courageous. School culture becomes infused with curiosity, laughter, and pride. Standardized tests may not capture it, but any hallway filled with joy, belonging, and purpose is proof that real learning is happening—and that's a standard worth raising.

Learned Skills: Practice Meets Purpose

While talents may start with natural inclination, *learned skills* are forged through effort. These are the competencies honed through training, repetition, and—let's be honest—a lot of on-the-job improvisation, especially if you've ever tried to master a new classroom tech tool five minutes before the bell rings.

Learned skills expand what we're capable of. They allow us to navigate a wide range of challenges with confidence—or at least a solid Plan B and a fistful of sticky notes. From conflict resolution to data analysis, to the near-magical ability to unjam a copier with one hand while grading essays with the other, these skills make schools *run*.

They're also what helps a teacher adapt a lesson on fractions into a Minecraft-themed math quest. Or enable a principal to turn Monday morning mayhem into calm efficiency before the third-period tardy bell rings.

And when these skills are cultivated over time, they often evolve into something bigger. A teacher once overwhelmed by classroom tech becomes the resident "Wizard of Wi-Fi," leading professional development for peers. A school librarian picks up coding, launches a digital innovation lab, and suddenly becomes a community hero.

What begins as a *need* often becomes a *calling*. These learned abilities become bridges to creativity, innovation, and authentic purpose. They empower educators to solve real problems, engage real students, and pursue real passions.

And in the process, they build a kind of resilience that doesn't come from textbooks—it comes from teaching through fire drills, surviving noisy construction, and remembering the names of 120 students while completely forgetting what you needed at the grocery store.

Reflection
- What talents do you bring to your role in education?
- What talents have you expanded or honed in your career?
- What talents/skills are you currently trying to improve?
- How have your talents helped you navigate challenging situations?

Talent – Don't Fear It

Let's just preemptively respond to the emails we *know* are coming. They'll sound something like:

1. **"Doesn't focusing on talents create labels or fixed mindsets?"**

   Concern: Teachers or students may be "boxed in" by what they're told they're good at.

   Response: When done right, talent identification should be liberating, not limiting. Talents are a starting point, not a ceiling—they show where growth comes naturally, but they don't dictate a singular path.

2. **"What if a student's talents don't align with academic subjects?"**

   Concern: A student might shine in areas like humor, movement, or social intuition that aren't traditionally measured.

   Response: That's exactly *why* we need talent-based approaches. Recognizing strengths outside of standard metrics builds confidence and engagement, and helps students see how their unique gifts can connect to real-world success.

3. **"How do we balance talent development with standards and curriculum demands?"**

   Concern: Time constraints and testing pressure leave little room for exploring talents.

   Response: Talent development isn't *extra*—it's a powerful tool for engagement and differentiation. When students use their strengths to access the content, they often achieve standards more meaningfully and efficiently.

4. **"What if a teacher doesn't feel confident identifying talents?"**

   Concern: Not all educators feel equipped.

   Concern: Teachers may be skeptical of buzzwords that come and go.

   Response: Supporting innate talents is not a new idea—it's just often overlooked. At its core, it's about helping people do what they do best, more often, with more purpose. That's not a trend—it's good teaching.

5. **"Aren't we just praising what kids already do well instead of challenging them?"**

   Concern: Focusing on strengths might lead to coasting or a lack of rigor.

   Response: True strength-based teaching *starts* with talents, but it also pushes students to grow. The best challenges are built at the *edge* of their talent zones, where they feel both capable and stretched.

6. **"Isn't this just another education fad?"**

   Concern: Teachers may be skeptical of buzzwords that come and go.

   Response: Supporting innate talents is not a new idea—it's just often overlooked. At its core, it's about helping people do what they do best, more often, with more purpose.

   That's not a trend—it's good teaching.

Everyone has innate talents. Yes, *everyone*. Even the teacher who insists, *"I'm not really good at anything—except maybe organizing chaotic field trips and calming down middle schoolers in under five minutes."* (Spoiler: that's a talent.)

Natural strengths come in all shapes and forms. Some are flashy—perfect pitch, artistic brilliance, math wizardry. Others are quieter but just as powerful—like knowing how to fix the laminator on the first try or offering the perfect word at just the right moment. Whatever they look like, *talents deserve to be recognized, celebrated, and used to align each individual with their purpose and potential.*

Let's be clear: valuing talent doesn't discount the power of hard work, perseverance, or nurture. It *complements* them—like peanut butter and jelly, or binge-watching TV while pretending to lesson plan. Talents give you a natural starting point, but it's effort and environment that allow those talents to grow.

We've all seen it. A student with a spark of curiosity becomes a full-blown learner for life when paired with the right encouragement and a patient teacher. Or a teacher who never thought they had a creative bone surprises everyone (including themselves) by stealing the show in the school musical, just because someone handed them a paintbrush and said, *"Go for it."*

And remember, talent isn't limited to flashy gifts or childhood prodigies. Our definition includes inborn gifts, yes, but also developed skills and lived experiences. A student who's spent years caring for younger siblings may already be a natural in problem-solving, empathy, and leadership. A teacher who once struggled with math may now be *the best* at explaining it, precisely because they remember how confusion feels.

That's talent—*forged through experience.*

The Real Purpose of Talent

The bottom line? We're not using talent to measure worth. We're using it to help people understand *how they operate at their best.*

When we name and nurture those strengths, we unlock a level of engagement, confidence, and innovation that no standardized test could ever measure. Talent matters—but it matters most when it's paired with *growth, grit,* and a school culture that says:

We see what you're great at—and we're here to help you grow it.

Talents Build School Culture—and Spark Innovation

When schools intentionally recognize and cultivate talents, something amazing happens: innovation doesn't just appear—it *thrives*, not as a top-down initiative, but as a natural outgrowth of people being empowered to bring their whole selves to school.

In these cultures, identity is honored. Dignity is affirmed. And schools stop being buildings full of job descriptions and become ecosystems full of possibility.

This is what it looks like in practice:

- A tech-savvy educational assistant becomes the go-to digital guru, turning confusing app updates into actual instructional magic.
- A retired parent with an eye for design organizes a student art show so beautiful the staff wonders if they've accidentally walked into a museum.
- A teacher with a background in improv transforms Shakespeare into a classroom comedy, where even the quietest kids ask for speaking roles.
- Another educator brings in their love of gardening—and suddenly the school courtyard is bursting with tomatoes, laughter, and lessons about plant life cycles, ecosystems, and patience.

These aren't one-off moments. They're *expressions of a culture* that values strengths, welcomes authenticity, and sees every person as a potential innovator.

Strong schools don't just check boxes—they *build belonging*. They empower staff to use their talents not as extras, but as essentials. Because when people feel seen, supported, and encouraged to lead with their gifts, they don't just do their jobs—they *transform them*.

What other profession lets you use your talents like this, *every single day*? Where else can your juggling skills earn both a standing ovation and a better way to teach kinetic energy?

Education is one of the rare careers where your whole self—your quirks, passions, and gifts—*belong*. And it doesn't stop at the classroom door. When educators develop and share their talents, the ripple effect is real. You influence more than your students—you uplift your peers, shape school systems, and energize entire communities.

A district leader passionate about real-world relevance might drive a grading policy overhaul that reflects what students *actually know and can do*. A teacher deeply connected to the local community might build a mentorship pipeline with nearby businesses, helping students see the connection between their learning and their futures… and maybe even land a summer job that doesn't involve a deep fryer.

The Renewable Energy of Purpose

Imagine your life as a *renewable energy system*.

- **Talents** are the *solar panels*—quietly absorbing and generating energy, often without you realizing it.
- **Passions** are the *sunlight*—fueling your drive and lighting the way, even on cloudy days.
- **Values** are the *grid*, keeping you grounded and connected, channeling your energy toward what matters most.
- **Aspirations** are the *battery storage*—holding your power for the long haul, giving you momentum even when the system is strained.

Together, these elements generate *purpose*—and it's sustainable.

Just like in a great energy system, overloads happen. Circuits short. You burn out. But then—just as you're running low—a curious student asks the perfect question that reboots your entire outlook. Or a colleague hands you a piece of dark chocolate and says, *"Let's power back up."* That's the beauty of this work: you're never running on empty for long.

Purpose in Alignment

When educators apply their talents in alignment with their personal values and professional aspirations, something extraordinary happens: they create impact that lasts.

For example:

- A *commitment to fairness and inclusion*, paired with a talent for curriculum design, leads to lesson plans that reflect and honor diverse identities.
- A *passion for mentorship*, combined with a gift for relationship-building, inspires a school leader to launch a teacher residency program that supports new educators and reduces burnout.
- A middle school teacher with a *knack for humor* uses laughter to defuse tension and build trust, creating a classroom where students feel safe, seen, and free to take risks.

These alignments don't just deepen engagement. They make the work *fulfilling*—and more importantly, *sustainable*.

Still Searching? You're More Talented Than You Think

Struggling to name your talents?

That's okay. Start with what comes naturally. What feels effortless to you but not to others? What do colleagues rely on you for? What do students remember you for?

Talents come in many forms:

- Translating data into insights that others can act on
- Knowing *just* when to step in—and when to stay back
- Turning a routine lesson into an unforgettable moment
- Listening deeply, noticing what others miss, or building trust quickly
- Surviving a whole week with the copy machine, Wi-Fi, and cafeteria lines *all* working against you, and still showing up with a smile

These are not soft skills. They're *essential strengths*. When you begin to name and nurture them, you'll find that your energy doesn't just return—it *expands*.

So go ahead. Juggle flaming batons if you have to. Just remember: the most powerful energy source in any school is a purpose-driven educator who knows what they're great at—and chooses to share it.

Creative Talents	Verbal & Communication Talents
• Artistic sense (drawing, painting, design) • Musical ear or rhythm • Natural sense of color or aesthetics • Dance or movement fluidity • Inventiveness or idea generation • Creative writing • Improvisation • Craftsmanship • Innovation and idea generation	• Storytelling • Persuasive speaking • Vocabulary acquisition • Language mimicry • Expressive reading • Wit and humor • Clear articulation • Listening and comprehension • Relationship-building
Cognitive Talents	**Social & Emotional Talents**
• Quick thinking • Natural curiosity • Excellent memory • Pattern recognition • Abstract reasoning • Spatial awareness • Fast learner • Intuitive problem-solving • Mathematical intuition	• Empathy and compassion • Reading social cues • Comfort in social situations • Leadership presence • Ability to build trust quickly • Negotiation instincts • Conflict de-escalation • Intuitive understanding of others' emotions

Physical & Kinesthetic Talents	Organizational & Leadership Talents
• Athleticism or coordination • Manual dexterity (fine motor skills) • Physical endurance • Fast reflexes • Balance and agility • Hands-on problem solving (tinkering, fixing, building) • Natural posture and body control	• Sense of order and structure • Time management instincts • Ability to multitask effectively • Delegating or directing naturally • Decision-making confidence • Strategic vision • Initiative-taking • Natural responsibility or follow-through
Sensory & Perceptual Talents	Intuitive & Observational Talents
• Acute hearing, smell, or taste • Noticing small details others miss • Sharp observational skills • High sensory awareness (useful in art, food, fashion, or nature work)	• Attention to detail — spots the small things others miss • Emotional intuition — reads between the lines, senses shifts in tone or energy • Curiosity — a deep desire to understand how things work or why things are the way they are

Talents in educators (and students) show up in countless forms—some loud and unmistakable, others subtle and surprising. But make no mistake: educators are *walking bundles of talent*. On any given day, you might:

- Turn a cardboard box into a castle
- Transform a math lesson into a rap
- Turn a rainy-day recess into an interpretive dance performance

Your *verbal talents* shine when you break down complex ideas, read *The Cat in the Hat* like it's Shakespeare, or somehow convince a room full of twelve-year-olds that comma placement *really* matters.

Your *cognitive strengths* are on full display as you spot patterns (like who forgot their homework—again), troubleshoot on the fly, and remember every student's allergy, nickname, and seating preference.

Thanks to your *emotional intelligence*, you can sense a mood shift before it reaches the hallway and de-escalate middle school drama faster than a Netflix teen series.

Your *physical skills* help you coach, assemble bulletin boards with Olympic precision, or dodge rogue glue sticks mid-lesson. And let's not forget your *organizational wizardry*—juggling 42 tasks at once while still remembering to submit your timesheet and order the construction paper.

Oh—and your *intuitive gifts*? Those let you read facial expressions with uncanny accuracy. (Seriously, are you part psychic?)

All of these talents, visible and invisible, combine daily—not just to teach, but to *inspire, improvise,* and, yes, sometimes just *survive until lunch.*

Discussion Questions

- How does your school recognize and support educators' talents?
- What hidden talent do *you* have that you wish could be better utilized at school?
- How can your school create more opportunities for students to explore and develop their talents?
- Think about your colleagues—what unique talents do they display, and how do they enhance your school culture?

Living Intentionally: Talents as Tools for a Purposeful Life

Developing your talents isn't just about checking off goals or feeling good. It's about living a life that feels *aligned, impactful,* and *undeniably yours.*

When educators lean into their gifts—both natural and nurtured—teaching shifts from being a job to becoming a *calling,* it's no longer

Video

only about standards and assessments. It becomes about *legacy, influence, and joy*. When your talents align with your values and aspirations, something magical happens. You hit that sweet spot—*where what you love, what you're good at, and what the world needs all collide.*

Talents in Action

- A high school principal who is equal parts strategist and empath doesn't just write improvement plans—they build trust while leading change.
- A middle school teacher with comedic timing isn't just funny—they're crafting a classroom culture grounded in safety, connection, and joy.

Talents aren't just what we're born with. They're built over time. They're shaped by *practice, failure, success*, and those glorious "I can't believe that worked!" moments.

Talents become the scaffolding that supports your values, fuels your passions, and drives your aspirations.

Purpose Multiplied

And here's the powerful part: when you live and lead with intention—when your *talents* align with your *values*—you don't just grow. You become a *catalyst* for growth in others.

You model creativity, authenticity, and integrity. You show your students that fulfillment doesn't come from playing it safe. It comes from *stretching, falling forward*, and *leading with the heart*.

This is bigger than individual success. When people operate from their strengths, *communities thrive*. Talents don't just raise test scores. They boost confidence, transform school culture, and spark change.

Talent-powered purpose is contagious—and it's a gift that keeps giving. So ask yourself:

- What lights you up?
- What do you value most?
- What legacy do you want to leave?

Because when talents meet purpose, the impact echoes far beyond your classroom.

It shapes lives.

The continuous engagement with one's talents also ensures adaptability in changing environments. In today's rapidly evolving world, where new industries arise and old ones transform or fade, the ability to adapt one's skills to new challenges is invaluable. Those who can blend their natural talents with newly acquired skills are better equipped to navigate these changes, turning potential threats into opportunities for growth and innovation.

Furthermore, the societal impact of nurturing talents cannot be overstated. When individuals can operate at their highest potential, they contribute more effectively to their communities. The benefits range from economic, as people excel in their careers, to cultural and social, as diverse talents enrich the community's fabric. This contribution is critical for societal progress and cohesion, as it encourages a culture of excellence and fulfillment.

Classroom Strategies to Support and Develop Talents
1. Create Opportunities for Self-Discovery

- Talent Inventories: Use surveys, journals, or guided reflections that ask students about what they enjoy, what feels easy for them, and when they feel most confident.
- Multiple Intelligences Activities: Integrate Howard Gardner's theory into lesson plans (e.g., music, bodily-kinesthetic, logical-

mathematical tasks) so students can identify how they naturally learn and express themselves.

- Learning Style Exploration: Let students try different roles in group projects—writer, presenter, organizer, designer—to help them notice what feels most natural and energizing.

2. Differentiate Instruction Based on Strengths

- Choice Boards & Menus: Let students select from various task options that allow them to demonstrate understanding in a way that aligns with their strengths—drawing, building, writing, performing, etc.
- Project-Based Learning: Allow long-term projects with flexible formats so students can go deep into topics they are curious or passionate about.
- Tiered Assignments: Offer varied levels of complexity, letting students work at the edge of their abilities to push growth while using their strengths as a base.

3. Provide Strength-Based Feedback

- Name Specific Talents: Instead of just saying "good job," point out the talent behind the action—"You explained that so clearly. You have a gift for simplifying complex ideas."
- Celebrate Progress Over Perfection: Help students see how refining their natural abilities is a journey, reinforcing that talent grows with effort and intention.
- Use Student Conferences: One-on-one conversations allow for deeper reflection and personalized guidance on talent development.

4. Build a Classroom Culture That Honors Individual Strengths

- "Talent Spotlights" or "Genius Hours": Dedicate time for students to explore and present a personal interest or skill.
- Peer Appreciation Moments: Allow students to recognize each other's strengths in structured ways, such as "compliment circles" or talent shoutouts.

- Visible Strength Boards: Create a wall display where students contribute examples of what they're good at and what they're working to improve.

5. Connect Talents to Real-World Roles

- Career Exploration Tied to Talents: Help students link what they enjoy doing now with future possibilities (e.g., "You love sports—have you thought about physical therapy, broadcasting, or sports marketing?").
- Invite Guest Speakers: Bring in professionals from diverse fields to discuss how their talents show up in their work.
- Service-Learning Projects: Allow students to apply their talents to community challenges, helping them see the impact of their abilities.

The best classrooms make space for *self-discovery*. Whether through talent inventories or a moment of realizing, *"Hey, I'm weirdly good at organizing group chaos"*, these environments help students see themselves clearly.

Differentiated instruction ensures flexibility, because not every student wants to write a paper when they could build a LEGO model of Ancient Rome.

Strength-based feedback tells students their talents aren't just "fun facts"—they're *meaningful assets*. Try: "You made that concept so engaging. Have you considered becoming a TED Talk prodigy?"

When we *celebrate strengths out loud*—with talent spotlights, shoutouts, or classroom displays—we create a culture where learning isn't just about knowledge. It's about *identity and ownership*. And when students connect their talents to the real world through service projects or guest speaker inspiration? That's when the dots connect between who they are now and who they're becoming.

Because let's be honest: the student who turns a group project into a full-scale Broadway production? That might be your future CEO. Or the next great drama teacher. Either way...

Talent wins.

The Ripple Effect of Talent-Driven Leadership

When we nurture talent—our own and that of others—we don't just build better classrooms or stronger schools. We build momentum. We light sparks in people who didn't know they could shine. Like the shy librarian who once swore public speaking wasn't her thing—until she read aloud in full costume at a school-wide event and had students cheering for chapter two like it was the Super Bowl.

Those sparks matter. They travel far beyond school walls—into homes, communities, and futures we may never fully witness but will always shape.

School leaders hold the rare and powerful privilege of creating space for those sparks. Sometimes that looks like formal professional development. But often, it's far simpler and more personal. Like saying, *"You crushed that parent night. You have a real gift for connection—can we build on that?"* Or noticing that the custodian who hums through the halls once played in a jazz band, and inviting them to co-lead the school talent show. It might mean tapping the administrative assistant with a laser focus on details to streamline school-wide communication (and save everyone from drowning in emails).

Talent-driven leadership is not about squeezing more out of people—it's about unlocking more *in* them. It's walking the halls with curiosity, not just a clipboard. It's leading meetings that ask, *"What strengths showed up?"* instead of only, *"What did the data say?"*

When school leaders shift from managing systems to cultivating ecosystems, they create living, breathing cultures where every person has a role, a rhythm, and a reason to belong. It's less about forcing people into molds and more about sculpting something far richer—a shared culture of purpose, connection, and belief.

So, keep asking the big questions:

What's working?

What's quietly waiting to be discovered?

And how can we help others not just *find* their talents, but *believe* in them?

Because the most powerful schools don't just teach—they ignite. And the most impactful leaders don't just manage—they empower. Whether you're launching bold initiatives or just navigating a copier jam with grace, your leadership is a spark. The future is already in your classrooms. Lead like it.

Supporting Educator Talents: A Blueprint for Thriving Schools

Supporting teacher talent isn't just good leadership—it's a smart strategy. It makes your school stronger, your team happier, and yes, it might even reduce complaints.

Start with discovery: use talent inventories, one-on-one conversations, or surveys that ask, *"What lights you up?"* or *"What feels like play instead of work?"* Align roles with strengths—so the spreadsheet-loving science teacher helps with budget reviews, not field day logistics (unless they love that too).

Amplify educator voices and talents consistently, not just during observations. Celebrate them in newsletters, announcements, or staff meetings. Shout out to the quiet art teacher who built the new school website over the weekend. Celebrate genius that hides in plain sight.

Then, make professional development personal. Offer options aligned with passion—trauma-informed instruction, creative assessments, student-led inquiry, or even how to build a classroom escape room. Let teachers lead their own learning—pilot projects, co-teaching labs, or "Genius Hour" for staff.

Want to build trust fast? Give strength-based feedback that's real and specific. Try, *"Your pacing is smoother than our new copier,"* instead of a generic *"Nice job."*

Encourage cross-pollination: pair the curriculum guru with the classroom culture rockstar to co-plan an unforgettable unit. Help teachers connect their gifts to the wider world—think service projects, local partnerships, or presenting at conferences (and yes, post about it like a proud parent on social media).

But most of all, build psychological safety. Model vulnerability. Celebrate effort over perfection. Normalize mistakes (yes, even lunch schedule fails). When people feel safe, they try bold things—and that's where brilliance lives.

And finally, remove barriers that block brilliance. Cut the busywork. Simplify meetings. Ask often, *"What can I do to help you do more of what you're amazing at?"*

Because when educators operate from their strengths, everybody wins. Especially the students, who get to learn from someone who isn't just competent, but lit up by the work.

From Compliance to Contribution

This isn't just a list of best practices—it's a blueprint for building a culture where talents don't just survive—they thrive. A culture where self-discovery is honored, opportunity is real, and autonomy is respected. Where feedback is meaningful, mentorship is intentional, and belonging is woven into every corner of the campus.

It's where a fifth grader discovers a passion for coding during Genius Hour, where a teacher rediscovers their creativity while leading a PD session on classroom design, where hallway conversations spark innovation, where smiles are just as common as standards.

Because school is more than schedules and benchmarks.

It's where hidden talents are spotlighted.

Where voices grow louder.

Where purpose comes to life.

And where teachers remember exactly why they signed up for this wild, wonderful work in the first place.

Talent: The Final Element

The journey to living with purpose is paved with four powerful elements: **Values, Passion, Aspirations**, and **Talents**. Each one brings dimension, direction, and a whole lot of color to your life's story—think less *gray cubicle*, more *hallway mural*. And if we're being honest? Talents are the glue that sticks. Sometimes glittery. Sometimes dried up and missing its cap. But always essential to holding it all together.

When your talents are in sync with your values, work doesn't just get done—it *matters*. Picture a STEM teacher who values curiosity and has a talent for hands-on problem solving. They're not just teaching engineering concepts—they're turning the classroom into a mini-innovation lab. Students learn by tinkering, failing, laughing, and trying again. A lesson on circuits becomes a confidence-building experience. The kid who usually shuns group work? They're suddenly leading the charge—with a cardboard robot in tow.

Now imagine a principal who values innovation and has a strange-but-amazing gift for spreadsheets. They're not just building dashboards. They're using data to advocate for student voice, staff wellness, and—let's be honest—more recess (which we all support).

Values act as your compass. They guide *how* you use your talents, *where* you say "yes," and *when* you bravely say "no thanks—that doesn't align." And when talents are paired with passion (the thing that wakes you at 3 a.m. with a bulletin board idea) and aimed toward aspirations (whether it's launching a district initiative or simply surviving the week with joy intact), the result is magic.

Or, at the very least, *controlled chaos with purpose*, which, in education, is basically the same thing.

This alignment doesn't just *feel* good—it fuels real, lasting impact. Talented educators who are lit up by their work shape futures, not just lesson plans. They create classrooms where students feel seen, valued, and challenged. They lead PD that's actually useful. They mentor others, not because they have to, but because they genuinely want to help someone else find their spark.

And here's the best part: this cycle of purpose-driven work doesn't burn out—it *renews*. The more you lead with your strengths, the more energy, motivation, and joy you find in the work. It's renewable energy—education's quiet superpower.

So take the time. Explore your talents. Polish them. Share them. Use them boldly.

Because the world doesn't need a slightly edited version of someone else.

It needs *you*—your full-hearted, authentic contribution.

Delivered with all the brilliance, humor, and quirky hallway dance moves only you can bring.

Especially in education, your one-of-a-kind combination of talents might be the very thing that helps a student finally feel like they belong, or helps a fellow teacher find the courage to try something new.

Purpose isn't a destination—it's a way of showing up.

So show up as you. Fully. Joyfully. With all your weird, wonderful, wildly valuable gifts.

Activity

Cultivating Talent: Next Steps for School Leaders

Are you a school leader? Then you're also a *talent scout*—whether you meant to be or not.

Creating a culture that supports educator talent starts with giving staff the time, space, and tools to name what comes naturally. Encourage teachers to reflect on what energizes them, what they're known for, and what they do so effortlessly that they forget it's special. Use tools like the *Talent Audit* (Appendix G) to spark these conversations.

Then take it one step further: amplify those gifts.

- Invite the tech-savvy teacher to co-lead a digital learning initiative.

- Ask the artistic educator to help redesign the school's visual identity.
- Tap the improv-loving teacher to energize your next all-staff meeting.
- Celebrate the quiet wins, the hidden gifts, and the unexpected brilliance that blooms when people are trusted to lead from their strengths.

When school leaders model this—by sharing their own talents, giving credit publicly, and redesigning roles to reflect strengths—they create a culture where talent is not just recognized, but *respected* and *put to work.*

Talent in Action: Examples That Spark Schoolwide Growth
- **Design for Pride**: Recognize a teacher's eye for aesthetics and invite them to co-create a staff lounge that's not just functional, but inspiring. The result? A ripple effect of ownership and schoolwide pride.
- **Music for Mornings**: Notice a staff member's musical ability and encourage them to start a morning music club. Bonus: student engagement goes up, and sleepy faces go down.
- **Mentorship Through Rapport**: Identify a paraprofessional's natural connection with students and pair them with newer staff to help build classroom culture, turning informal talent into intentional mentorship.
- **Kickoff with Purpose**: Use your own storytelling talent to open staff meetings with quick, reflective anecdotes that center purpose and humor, rather than just bell schedules.
- **Map What Matters**: Lean into your strategic strength by leading staff through a talent-mapping exercise. Help teams align responsibilities with what they do best—because no one thrives doing what drains them.

Celebrate unique staff talents publicly, from the cafeteria manager's recipe hacks to the custodian's impeccable bulletin board trimming, reinforcing that everyone's strengths contribute to the school's success, not just test scores.

Encourage a teacher with community connections to form partnerships with local businesses, opening doors to student internships and service-learning opportunities that bring the curriculum to life.

Classroom Lessons

Invite a tech-savvy teacher to lead mini-PD sessions, building internal leadership capacity while saving the school from one more outside consultant who doesn't know how to work the projector.

Are you a teacher? Then you already know your classroom is full of hidden talents—some obvious, some still waiting to be discovered between bathroom breaks and pencil sharpener lineups. We invite you to use these lessons (Appendix H) to help students explore their unique talents—the things they do naturally, joyfully, and sometimes without even realizing they're special. These activities are designed to spark conversations like, "Wait, organizing our group project *was* kind of fun," or "I didn't know being a good listener was a talent!" Helping students recognize their strengths is like handing them a mirror and saying, "Look at you go." Whether it's building confidence, fueling creativity, or identifying that one student who can turn any topic into a rap battle, you're helping kids see what's *right* with them—and how that can grow. So, dive in. Ask what lights them up. Laugh when someone insists their talent is burping the alphabet (you never know, future voice actor?). And remind them often: their talents aren't just quirks—they're clues. Clues that point to possibility, purpose, and the kind of future that feels uniquely theirs.

Voices from the Field

> Teaching 9th grade is not for the faint of heart—but luckily, one of my hidden talents is surviving daily chaos with humor and grace (and a lot of energy drinks). I've learned that if I can get a room full of 14-year-olds to laugh and learn something in the same 45 minutes, I'm doing my job. One of my strongest talents is connecting with students, especially the ones who walk in on day one convinced that high school is just middle school with more stress and worse lunches. I make it a point to break down walls, whether through bad puns, overly dramatic readings of the syllabus, or pretending I don't notice when someone says, "Wait, we had homework?" for the third day in a row. I also have a knack for translating complicated content into something that feels manageable—and dare I say, even fun.
>
> Whether I'm comparing literary themes to TikTok drama or turning math problems into pizza dilemmas, I use my creativity and a touch of ridiculousness to keep students engaged. But underneath the humor is a serious purpose: I want every student to feel seen, supported, and capable. Freshman year sets the tone, and I know I have the opportunity to either make it smoother or more stressful. I choose smoother, with some laughter along the way. My purpose is to help students find their footing, build their confidence, and realize that learning doesn't have to be intimidating—it can actually be awesome.

Remy (9th grader): Honestly, I never really thought of my talents as anything that deep until this year. I always knew I was good at helping people stay calm, explaining things in a way that makes sense, and making people laugh when things get stressful. I didn't think of that as a "talent," I just thought of it as being the person who tells dumb jokes before a test or helps someone figure out their homework five minutes before class. But now, as a senior, I realize those things are part of my purpose. I've become the person people come to when they're overwhelmed—friends, even underclassmen. I'm the one who can turn a group project meltdown into something that actually gets done (and with less drama). I guess my talent is bringing people together and keeping the vibe positive, even when school is tough. I've also figured out that I'm good at encouraging people. Whether it's hyping someone up before their presentation or reminding them that one bad grade isn't the end of the world, I like being that voice that says, "You've got this." It makes me feel like I'm actually making a difference, even if it's small.

So yeah, my purpose isn't just about getting good grades or choosing a major—I think it's about using what I'm naturally good at to help others feel supported. Whether I go into teaching, counseling, or something else, I know I want to keep doing that. I want people to leave a conversation with me feeling a little more confident than they did before.

Challenge: Add your voice to Talents. Email us at Purposestories@quagliainstitute.org and upload your story. Feel free to identify yourself and your school (or remain anonymous).

Talent Development Checklist for All School Personnel

Use this checklist to reflect on how you support talent discovery and growth within yourself, your students, and your professional community. Check all that apply.

Recognizing and Growing My Own Talents

- I regularly reflect on what I do naturally well—even if it doesn't always feel "special."
- I seek feedback from colleagues to help identify my hidden strengths and instincts.
- I invest time in developing my talents through practice, learning, or experimentation.
- I use my natural abilities and experiences to bring energy and excellence to my work.
- I view my talents as dynamic skills I can continue to grow, not fixed traits.

Supporting Student Talent Development

- I intentionally observe and note what students do with ease or joy.
- I create opportunities for students to use and showcase their talents in the classroom.
- I validate all types of talents—not just academic ones—including creativity, empathy, leadership, or humor.
- I design activities or assessments that allow students to express their strengths in diverse ways.
- I help students connect their talents to bigger goals, aspirations, and real-world possibilities.

Encouraging Talent in Colleagues

- I notice and name the talents I see in my coworkers, especially the ones they might not recognize.
- I invite team members to contribute based on their strengths in group projects or planning.
- I support professional development that helps staff identify and grow their unique talents.
- I create a culture where it's safe to try, fail, and stretch into new strengths.
- I celebrate the diverse talents that make our school stronger, even if they're not always visible.

Creating a Talent-Conscious School Culture

- I help foster an environment where talents are viewed as potential to be developed, not fixed labels.
- I recognize that lived experiences and learned skills are just as valuable as natural gifts.
- I encourage colleagues and students to reflect on how their talents can serve others and drive purpose.
- I share stories and examples of "talent in action" to inspire growth in my school community.
- I embrace the idea that everyone has something unique to contribute, and I look for it daily.

References

Allan, B. A., & Duffy, R. D. (2014). Examining moderators of signature strengths use and well-being: Calling and signature strengths level. *Journal of Happiness Studies, 15*(2), 323–337.

Douglass, R. P., & Duffy, R. D. (2015). Strengths use and life satisfaction: A moderated mediation approach. *Journal of Happiness Studies, 16*(3), 619–632.

Seligman, M. E., Ernst, R. M., Gillham, J., Reivich, K., & Linkins, M. (2009). Positive education: Positive psychology and classroom interventions. *Oxford Review of Education, 35*(3), 293–311.

Waters, L. (2015a). The relationship between strength-based parenting with children's stress levels and strength-based coping approaches. *Psychology, 6*(6), 689–698.

Waters, L. E. (2015b). Strength-based parenting and life satisfaction in teenagers. *Advances in Social Sciences Research Journal, 2*(11), 158–173.

06 | The Spark Within:

Fueling Life Through the Elements of Purpose

Educating the mind without educating
the heart is no education at all.

– Aristotle

We hope you're starting to understand why we believe purpose is everything for educators. When teaching is anchored in a clear sense of purpose, it shifts from a daily grind into a meaningful adventure. You're no longer just showing up—you're stepping into something bigger. You're on a mission. You have a *why,* and that *why* fuels you. It keeps you coming back with energy, even on the days when third period has already drained you. Purpose helps you bounce back after a tough class, uplift your students when they're discouraged, and find joy in small victories, like when a quiet student finally raises their hand, or when the whole class turns in their homework on time.

Think of it this way: without purpose, teaching can feel like rowing a boat with no destination. You're moving, yes—but are you getting anywhere meaningful? Purpose gives direction. It ties who you are to the impact you want to leave behind. It fills your days with deeper meaning—meaning that stretches far beyond the walls of the classroom.

Now, let's explore how *Values, Passions, Aspirations,* and *Talents* come together to ignite and sustain this sense of purpose. This is crucial because it allows us to recognize—and celebrate—the unique strengths and stories each person brings to the table. It invites us to redefine success. It's not just about test scores anymore. It's about how people use their gifts and passions to grow, reach their goals, and make a difference in the world.

As educators, it's our responsibility to build classrooms where these qualities can thrive. Our job isn't just to teach facts—it's to help students dream big, think creatively, and lead with heart. When we do this well, we're equipping them to make wise choices and bold contributions—choices that reflect their deepest values and ripple out into their communities and beyond.

Values are your non-negotiables—the bedrock beliefs that shape how you live and teach. Maybe you believe every student deserves a fair shot, no matter their background. Maybe your foundation is built on integrity, equity, or excellence, pushing students to exceed even their own expectations. Whatever your core values are, when they align with your purpose, something powerful happens. You teach with authenticity. You build real trust. You create a space where students feel safe to reflect on and develop their own values, too.

Passion is the emotional rocket fuel that propels purpose. It's the spark behind the science teacher who lights up while explaining chemical reactions or the history teacher who goes all-in crafting a cardboard Roman Colosseum. Passion makes the hard work not just bearable, but exciting. When your students see your real excitement—whether it's for a subject, their growth, or life itself—they absorb it. Passion transforms learning into an adventure. And when your purpose is powered by passion, it becomes contagious. The energy spreads, infusing the classroom, the faculty room, and even the community. That emotional investment is what creates a vibrant space where curiosity thrives and enthusiasm is the norm.

Aspirations are the dreams you carry forward—the long-term goals that keep you moving. Maybe you want to shift your school's culture toward creativity and collaboration. Maybe you aim to mentor the next generation of educators or champion bold reforms that change the system. Purpose acts as the bridge between where you are and where you hope to be. It takes what feels like a distant goal and turns it into purposeful, day-by-day momentum. Aspirations help you weather change, anchor your growth, and remind you that every step—however small—is part of something much bigger.

Talents are your personal strengths—the skills, instincts, and learned abilities that make your teaching style your own. Maybe, like Mel Blanc, you've got a gift for mimicking voices that keeps your students hanging on every word. Maybe you're the tech-savvy teacher who makes digital learning feel like play. Or maybe you have the calm, steady presence that can defuse conflict with a look or a single word. When your purpose draws on your talents, everything begins to click. You're no longer trying to fit into someone else's idea of what a "great teacher" should be. You're teaching from the core of who you are. That authenticity boosts your effectiveness, confidence, and influence—because you're doing what you do best, in service of something meaningful.

When *Values*, *Passions*, *Aspirations*, and *Talents* align, purpose stops being just a concept. It becomes something you live, something you embody. It becomes the thread weaving together your identity, your intentions, and your impact. And when that happens—when your teaching flows from a place of true purpose—it becomes more than a job. It becomes a calling. A force for change. Something that shapes not just your students' lives, but your own.

Losing the Spark: How Missing Elements Weaken Purpose

While aligning purpose with the four elements builds a rock-solid foundation for educators, each element plays a vital role in shaping who we are and how we show up in the world. When one of those elements is missing, it's like the lights dim a little, making everything harder to navigate. The good news? Recognizing what's missing isn't a sign of failure—it's an invitation. An opportunity to pause, reflect, and reignite your inner spark.

Let's explore how these gaps can show up—and more importantly, how we can find our way back to purpose. Whether it's a lack of clear values, fading passion, unacknowledged aspirations, or underutilized talents, these disconnects often lead to burnout, frustration, and a sense of emotional drift. But when we examine these misalignments closely, we begin to notice the signs—and from there, we can take intentional steps to realign with what truly matters.

This is how we restore meaning to our efforts. This is how we re-energize our commitment to both personal fulfillment and the greater good.

Directionless Purpose: The Void of Unclear Values

Imagine trying to drive cross-country without a GPS—or even an old-fashioned road map. (And yes, many of us remember navigating without digital help!) That's what life feels like without clear values. Values are your internal compass. When they're missing, decision-making becomes like throwing darts blindfolded. You might hit something… but probably not what you intended.

Without clearly defined values, people often feel unsure about what's right or wrong in any given situation. There's no consistent guide, so choices get fuzzy. Instead of responding with clarity, people start reacting impulsively. One day it's yes, the next it's no, and even they aren't sure why. This back-and-forth behavior leads to confusion, and not just for others, but for themselves. Over time, it chips away at trust.

Trust is built on predictability—the belief that someone will act with consistency and integrity. But when a person seems to drift without a moral anchor, it's hard for others to know where they stand. That unpredictability creates cracks in relationships, like a sidewalk splintered by a hard winter freeze.

Even success can feel hollow when values aren't in place. You might reach the top of a mountain, only to realize it wasn't your mountain—it was someone else's idea of success. Without the grounding force of personal values, achievement loses its meaning.

There's another danger, too: vulnerability to outside voices. When values aren't clear, people tend to absorb the beliefs or goals of those around them, just to fit in, avoid conflict, or chase approval. Choices get made based on other people's expectations, not one's own truth. And slowly, without even realizing it, individuals may stop questioning decisions that don't align with their school's mission—or with the reason they got into education in the first place.

This leads to a deeper, quieter erosion. The more someone acts in ways that don't align with their authentic self, the more they feel disconnected. They may begin to question not just their decisions, but their identity. *Who am I in all of this? What do I actually believe?* That dissonance, left unchecked, becomes emotional fatigue. Purpose slips away. Fulfillment fades.

But here's the truth: this kind of misalignment isn't the end. It's a signal. And if we're willing to pay attention, it's the first step toward rediscovery. Reconnecting with your values is like turning the lights back on. It brings clarity, direction, and the confidence to navigate with purpose, no matter how long you've been drifting.

Think of an educator who's passionate about innovation but finds themselves trapped in a system laser-focused on test scores. Without grounding values, they might start to *just go along to get along,* slowly losing sight of why they entered the classroom in the first place. Over time, they stop questioning policies, stop pushing boundaries, and simply follow the script—even when it contradicts their instincts.

In short: **Values = Alignment.** Without them, it's easy to drift, doubt yourself, or chase validation from the outside rather than fulfillment from within. A lack of clear values stunts personal growth and dims the light of meaningful contribution. Values help define not only who we are, but also *how* we engage with the world. When those guiding principles are missing, the foundation of purpose begins to crack, impacting everything from our decisions and direction to our relationships and our sense of self.

From Inspired to Exhausted: The Cost of Lost Passion

Passion is what makes the hard days worth it. It's the secret ingredient that turns *just another Tuesday* into a *this is why I do this* kind of day. Without passion, even the simplest tasks start to feel endless. What was once fulfilling becomes draining. Engagement drops. Joy fades.

Think about the teacher who used to spend Sunday nights crafting exciting, student-centered projects—now they just copy worksheets from a folder because *it's good enough*. Picture the once-enthusiastic drama teacher who stayed late rehearsing every line with students, now simply handing out scripts and counting the days to closing night. Or the coach who used to invent creative practice drills, now stuck on autopilot, feeling more like a referee than a mentor.

When passion fades, emotional investment disappears. Grading papers, supervising lunch duty, attending meetings—these once-manageable routines become heavy, joyless chores. What once felt energizing becomes exhausting. That spark? It flickers. Productivity dips. Satisfaction slips. And before long, the days feel less like a calling and more like a countdown.

This kind of disengagement doesn't just wear you down—it derails your direction. Passion gives purpose a heartbeat. It's what propels people toward meaningful goals. Without it, focus blurs. Motivation weakens. You're still showing up, but you're not sure what you're working toward anymore. That sense of drifting—of going through the motions without a clear why—leads to frustration and fatigue.

Passion is also deeply connected to identity. It shapes how we see ourselves and what we believe we're meant to do. So, when passion fades, it shakes us. *If I'm not the enthusiastic teacher, the creative planner, the motivator... then who am I now?* Losing that connection can lead to a sense of confusion—and eventually, reinvention.

In the absence of passion, priorities often shift. Practical needs take the front seat—paychecks, schedules, security. And while these things *do* matter, they can quietly pull us away from what once inspired us. The change is subtle but significant. A person might be succeeding by all outward standards—and still feel empty on the inside.

But here's the hopeful truth: the absence of passion can be a powerful wake-up call. It can nudge us to explore. To try something new. To shake things up.

An educator feeling disconnected might join a professional learning cohort, mentor a student club, or volunteer for a new initiative. These small shifts can rekindle energy in unexpected ways. Others may take a leap—switching grade levels, moving into leadership, or rediscovering old creative outlets. Even a single new experience can open a door to a renewed sense of excitement and possibility.

This period of search—while sometimes uncomfortable—is often where real growth begins. In exploring new paths, many educators discover fresh passions that redefine their purpose. And in doing so, they don't just reignite their spark—they illuminate a whole new direction.

When Purpose Fades: Living Without Aspirations

Aspirations serve as the bridge between who we are today and who we hope to become. They exist in two essential dimensions: *dreaming* and *doing*. Dreaming invites us to envision a future rich with possibilities. Doing brings that vision to life through tangible steps. When either part is missing—when someone stops imagining what's possible or lacks the momentum to act—aspiration loses its power. Without it, individuals often feel unmotivated, stagnant, or adrift.

In education, this disconnection might look like a once-hopeful teacher who dreamed of creating a dynamic, student-centered classroom but now sticks rigidly to the curriculum, feeling handcuffed by policy or pressure. Or consider the principal who once envisioned transforming their school into a beacon of innovation and community, but now spends most days buried in compliance reports, the original dream slowly fading into the background.

Dreaming fuels motivation. It brings energy, hope, and a reason to press forward. When the ability to dream is lost, everyday efforts start to feel disconnected from any larger vision. That missing sense of purpose leads to disengagement, and goals that once mattered begin to quietly slip away. Picture the elementary science teacher who once dreamed of launching a space exploration club. After years of budget cuts, standardized testing, and administrative roadblocks, they stopped submitting new proposals. Their passion dims—not just for the club, but for teaching itself.

Then there's *doing*, the second dimension of aspiration. Doing gives structure and forward motion. It transforms possibility into reality. But without the drive—or even the clarity—to take action, even the most inspired visions stay stuck on paper. When educators feel overwhelmed or unsure how to start, they may freeze. Over time, inaction leads to a sense of stagnation. Progress fades. Accomplishments feel scarce. And without aspirations, there are no clear benchmarks to measure growth or celebrate success. This absence can chip away at a person's self-worth and confidence.

Aspirations also anchor internal direction. Without them, people become more susceptible to outside influences. Instead of chasing dreams that align with their values, they chase accolades, promotions, or approval. They say yes to every district initiative—not because it resonates, but because they're unsure of what *they* truly want. The result? A once-creative teacher who now plays it safe to avoid criticism. A department head who pursues an administrative path not because it excites them, but because it's "the next logical step." Without their own aspirations to guide them, they end up following someone else's map.

The emotional toll of lost aspirations can be profound without a sense of *why*, life starts to feel like a checklist of tasks instead of a meaningful journey. That lack of forward motion can lead to feelings of anxiety, low self-esteem, or even depression. Mental well-being depends on direction and momentum—two things that aspirations consistently provide.

In both teaching and leadership, aspirations matter. For educators, dreaming is what helps them imagine the impact they want to make. Doing is what turns those visions into actual outcomes. When aspiration fades, it's not just personal fulfillment that's at risk—it's the ability to inspire others. Teachers model possibility. When they stop dreaming and doing, that loss of vision echoes into their classrooms and staffrooms.

The true power of aspiration lies in the balance between dreaming and doing:

- *Dreaming without doing* becomes fantasy—all vision, no traction.
- *Doing without dreaming* becomes routine—all motion, no meaning.

But when both work together, they generate purpose. When an educator dares to dream of launching an arts program *and* takes action to bring it to life, energy returns. Confidence builds. Momentum grows. And suddenly, the road ahead feels not only visible, but exciting.

Untapped Potential: When Talents Go Unseen

Talents—our natural gifts, learned skills, and lived experiences—are vital resources in shaping our purpose and achieving meaningful goals. When these strengths go unrecognized or underdeveloped, frustration sets in. People begin to doubt themselves. Their internal compass falters. Even small challenges start to feel overwhelming, and confidence begins to erode.

In schools, this often shows up in students whose strengths don't match conventional academic measures. It might look like a student doodling comic strips in the margins of a math test, dismissed as distracted when, in reality, they're bursting with creativity. Or a middle schooler who constructs elaborate digital worlds in Minecraft, showing early signs of engineering talent that go unnoticed because no one thought to ask or look deeper.

When talents are overlooked, students internalize failure. They begin to question their value. They stop raising their hands. Stop taking risks. Stop dreaming altogether. This silent erosion can follow them into adulthood, where untapped strengths continue to gather dust, leaving purpose unexplored and potential unrealized.

But when talents are noticed, nurtured, and channeled, everything changes. Confidence builds. Possibilities open. And that quiet, often hidden light? It starts to shine.

The Consequences of Unseen Talents

Without a foundation of skills, individuals often encounter limited opportunities. In nearly every sphere—professional, academic, or personal—skills serve as the currency of access. Without them, doors remain closed. People are left standing outside, watching others advance, unsure of how to move forward themselves. This lack of access doesn't just stall progress; it erodes confidence, blurs direction, and weakens the very sense of fulfillment that purpose provides.

When talents go underdeveloped or unrecognized, individuals face a cascade of challenges:

- **Frustration and self-doubt:** Struggling to identify or grow one's talents can create deep internal conflict. When repeated efforts fail to gain traction, confidence starts to slip. Over time, even small challenges can feel insurmountable. *Maybe I'm just not good enough* becomes a dangerous and defeating thought loop.

- **Limited opportunities:** In a world where skills open doors, lacking the right ones can leave people locked out. Opportunities for growth, advancement, or recognition may pass by, not because of a lack of potential, but because that potential was never supported or developed. Without access, individuals lose momentum. They begin to question if their goals are even reachable.

- **Dependence on others:** While collaboration is essential, excessive reliance on others can feel disempowering. When individuals don't believe they can succeed on their own, autonomy suffers. This dependence chips away at their ability to fully embrace their own purpose, leading to feelings of inadequacy or invisibility.
- **Stalled progress toward goals:** Aspirations need tools. Without the skills to bring a dream to life, even the most inspiring goals can start to feel impossible. When big visions meet underdeveloped talents, dreams stall. The result? Discouragement. Repeatedly hitting walls rather than milestones can wear down belief in the value of the goal itself.
- **Social withdrawal:** Feeling untalented or "less than" can affect how individuals show up in group settings. If someone believes they have nothing valuable to contribute, they may begin to shrink into the background. Over time, they withdraw from conversations, collaboration, and connection. But purpose thrives in a relationship. Without meaningful interaction, it's harder to feel seen—and harder still to feel like you matter.
- **Mental health challenges:** The long-term emotional toll of unrecognized or undeveloped talents is real. Persistent feelings of inadequacy can fuel anxiety, depression, and disconnection. A person who once had a spark now feels stuck, uncertain, and unseen.

Hidden in Plain Sight

We often talk about talents as if they're buried treasure—hidden deep, waiting to be uncovered. But more often, they're right in front of us. Hidden in plain sight.

A student who always takes the lead in group projects may have natural leadership potential, but because their test scores aren't stellar, no one notices. A quiet child who listens intently and shares thoughtful insights may possess remarkable emotional intelligence—yet remains invisible in a system that rewards speed and volume over depth and reflection.

Talents also stay hidden when students don't see themselves represented. Imagine being a first-generation college student who excels at public speaking—but has never heard of a debate team, a TEDxYouth event, or a local youth council. Representation and access matter. We can't pursue what we don't know exists.

Creating Space for Talent to Grow

To unlock talent, we must first create environments where it can be seen. This means shifting how we teach, what we assess, and what we celebrate. Education should be less about sorting students into categories and more about supporting them in their strengths.

Purpose grows where talents are nurtured. And it doesn't take much to make that happen: a teacher who says, *"You're really good at that,"* a classroom that allows trial and error without penalty, or a project that taps into a student's interests beyond the textbook. These moments may seem small, but they are the seeds of transformation.

When students are allowed to explore, fail, try again, and stretch their limits, talents begin to surface. They stop hiding. They grow. The absence of visible skills doesn't mean the absence of purpose. It simply means the right environment for discovery hasn't been created yet.

With encouragement, intentional design, and safe spaces to try—and-try again, every learner has the capacity to uncover their potential and move toward a purposeful life.

It's Not a Deficit—It's a Delay

It's also essential to understand that what appears to be a lack of talent is often just a lack of opportunity. Many untapped strengths exist not because they don't exist, but because they were never given the chance to emerge.

Some students don't know they're gifted speakers because they've never been asked to present. Others could be brilliant problem-solvers, but no one ever handed them a real-world problem. Talents need space, exposure, and support. Without them, students—and adults—miss out on discovering what they're capable of.

So let's reframe the narrative. An undeveloped skill isn't a failure. It's a delayed bloom. A path blocked, not a path erased. With time, care, and opportunity, growth is always possible. Everyone has the potential to evolve. Everyone deserves a chance to shine.

Here is the developmentally edited version of your passage:

If we want every student to feel a sense of purpose, we must be intentional about helping them see what they're capable of. That means broadening our definition of talent, removing the blinders imposed by rigid systems, and giving every learner the space to explore, stumble, grow, and try again. Because when talents go unseen, potential goes untapped. And when potential goes untapped, it's not just the individual who loses—*the entire world misses out* on what could have been.

Igniting Purpose: Uniting the Core Elements of Who You Are

In the end, purpose isn't a final destination—it's a lifelong road trip. It's not something you find once and hold onto forever. It's shaped and reshaped over time by the alignment of four powerful, living elements: *Values, Passions, Aspirations,* and *Talents.* These are not fixed points. They evolve as we grow, stumble, recover, succeed, and reimagine who we are and what we're meant to do.

For educators, purpose begins with knowing who you are and what you stand for. It is sustained by the daily choice to teach, lead, and live with intention—even on the days when nothing goes as planned.

When these four elements are nurtured and in harmony, purpose becomes more than an abstract idea. It becomes a steady, driving force. It's the quiet nudge that compels an exhausted teacher to stay after school to support a struggling student. It's the spark that inspires a counselor to launch a new initiative for at-risk youth, even when their schedule is overflowing. It's the vision that pushes a principal to advocate fiercely for funding, even when the odds are long.

Purpose anchors our work in something deeper than lesson plans or policy checklists. It turns teaching from a profession into a calling, and transforms learning from a task into a legacy.

Of course, the path to purpose isn't always smooth. There will be moments when one or more of these elements feels distant, disconnected, or unclear. Times when everything feels out of sync. Moments when your values feel compromised and you start questioning if you're still aligned with what matters most. Times when your passion feels like a memory, buried under the weight of grading, meetings, and late-night lesson plans. Seasons when aspirations fade—when changing the world gets replaced by just trying to make it through Friday. Or when your talents go unseen—not because they don't exist, but because the environment hasn't allowed them to shine.

These are not signs of failure. They are invitations—gentle calls to pause, breathe, and pay attention. They ask the hard but necessary questions:

What do I believe in? What makes me come alive? What am I working toward that still excites me? What can I offer that no one else quite can?

Through reflection, we begin the quiet, courageous work of rebuilding our connection to purpose, stronger, clearer, and more resilient than before.

It's essential to remember: *living with purpose does not mean living perfectly.* It means living awake. Living intentionally. Purpose doesn't demand constant passion or flawless execution. It asks only that we stay aware—aware of when we drift, and willing to realign.

It's about noticing what's missing, being honest about it, and taking the small, brave steps to find it again. This imperfect journey—with all its detours and redirections—is what gives purpose its power. It's what makes it *real.*

Educators who embrace this process model see something profound. They show students and colleagues that struggle isn't something to hide—it's something to grow from. That purpose isn't a treasure we discover and then hold onto—it's something we *return to*, again and again, with greater wisdom each time.

When our values guide decisions, when passion brings energy to our work, when aspirations point toward a meaningful future, and when talents empower us to contribute in ways only we can, purpose becomes a lived experience. It weaves identity into action. It turns potential into impact. It transforms ordinary moments into moments of deep influence.

And in that space—where heart, clarity, and talent meet—educators don't just teach. *They lead. They lift. They ignite transformation.*

Reconnecting to What Matters

When we reconnect with our *Values, Passions, Aspirations,* and *Talents,* we don't just refuel ourselves—we uplift everyone around us. Purpose-driven educators create classrooms where students feel seen, heard, and challenged to grow. They build schools that are not just centers of instruction, but spaces of creativity, courage, and belonging.

Living and leading with purpose isn't about rare, grand moments. It's in the daily, often quiet, choices we make. It's in greeting students by name. In modeling curiosity and courage. In offering grace when someone falls short. Purpose is not a performance. It's a presence.

If you're wondering where to begin, try this:

- **Reflect regularly.** Ask what feels aligned, and what needs attention.
- **Revisit your "why."** Let it evolve as you do.
- **Seek spaces that nourish you.** Surround yourself with people who challenge, support, and uplift you.
- **Be patient with the process.** Purpose is not built in a day. It's strengthened one honest choice at a time.

As you move forward, remember: your purpose isn't just about what you do. It's about *how* you do it—with heart, with courage, and with an open hand toward others.

Every step you take, every moment of realignment, contributes to something far greater than a job description. You don't just teach curriculum. You teach *hope*. *Resilience*. The courage to become.

And that—that is where real transformation begins.

07 | Shaping Tomorrow:

How Purpose-Driven Educators Can Redefine Education

> *There is no passion to be found playing small - in settling for a life that is less than the one you are capable of living.*
>
> — **Nelson Mandela**

Imagine a school where the bell doesn't just signal the start of another class—it rings in *possibility*, *creativity*, and *mission*. In this reimagined landscape of education, classrooms are alive with curiosity, laughter, and a collective sense of purpose. Teachers aren't simply delivering lessons; they're igniting minds, connecting ideas, and shaping the next generation of thinkers, doers, and dreamers.

In this future, purpose-driven educators teach with a clear and compelling "why" behind every plan. Their work transcends content delivery—they become mentors, visionaries, and changemakers. Even a Tuesday morning math class becomes a launchpad for real-world problem-solving. These educators infuse intention into every interaction, creating experiences that don't just prepare students for tests, but for *life*, with all its complexities, challenges, and promise.

Schools in this model are not institutions. They are ecosystems. Alive with innovation, voice, and a bold belief that education isn't just about learning facts—it's about changing lives.

Engaged Minds, Purposeful Learning

In the future we imagine, student engagement is no longer measured by quiet compliance or completed worksheets. It's seen in the spark in a student's eyes when a lesson suddenly feels relevant. Purposeful learning begins when students connect what they're learning to something that genuinely matters to them.

Here, teachers are more than experts—they're mentors, coaches, and co-learners. They foster meaningful exploration and deeper understanding. A science teacher might tie a unit on ecosystems to local environmental issues. A history teacher could connect civil rights movements to current global conversations about equity. Suddenly, education becomes a toolkit—not just for knowledge, but for impact.

Students in these classrooms are no longer passive receivers of information. They are engaged participants in their own growth. The result? Classrooms transform into vibrant, dynamic spaces. Curiosity drives instruction. Learning becomes an ongoing conversation between student and teacher, and inquiry becomes the fuel for real transformation.

Fueled by their own clarity of purpose, these educators bring their full selves into the classroom. They teach not just the "what," but the "why." A math teacher passionate about social justice might introduce data literacy through real-world statistics on income inequality. An English teacher grounded in emotional awareness might lead literature discussions that explore identity, empathy, and human experience.

These moments do more than inform—they *ignite*. Educators who align their personal values and passions with their instruction show students what it means to live and work with purpose. Their classrooms become mirrors and windows—reflecting students' lives while opening views into broader perspectives. Education becomes a dialogue, not a directive. A partnership, not a performance.

Learning That Resonates

Purposeful teaching transforms learning into a dynamic exchange where students are invited to follow their interests and pursue what excites them. A student with a passion for design might create an infographic in place of a traditional essay. A shy student might gain confidence by presenting a family heritage project that connects their personal story to a larger historical context.

Engagement becomes *personal*. It becomes profound.

And it grows because educators recognize the power of *individualization*. Purpose-driven teachers tailor instruction to highlight student strengths, passions, and goals. This approach ensures that education becomes more than an academic transaction—it becomes a journey of personal development.

Students learn more than facts. They learn who they are. They gain confidence. They cultivate awareness. And those are the qualities that carry far beyond the classroom—into careers, relationships, and communities.

In this model of education, everyone wins. Students thrive, not just as learners, but as whole people. Teachers find renewed joy in their work. And schools become the kinds of places where dreams are nurtured, talents are recognized, and purpose is both the foundation and the fuel.

Perhaps most powerfully, this model creates a shared vision between teachers and students. Education becomes more than a one-way transfer of knowledge—it becomes a collaborative, purpose-filled journey. In this environment, learners are encouraged to explore how their voices, talents, and decisions can contribute to a better world.

Picture a student launching a school-wide recycling campaign after studying environmental sustainability. Or another writing to a local official about a civic issue they explored in social studies. These aren't hypothetical scenarios—they're the natural outcomes of purpose-driven education. Classrooms become incubators for *action, understanding*, and *real-world change*.

In this model, the classroom transforms into a *community*—a space where students feel heard, seen, and empowered. Purpose-driven educators foster cultures where questions are welcomed, ideas are celebrated, and every student knows their presence matters. The classroom becomes a microcosm of society, where negotiation, collaboration, and innovation take root early and grow deep.

These daily interactions, anchored in purpose, prepare students not only to succeed academically but also to participate meaningfully in society. They develop a lasting belief that their contributions count—and that their voices can shape the world around them.

Purposeful Spaces: Crafting Environments That Inspire Learning

In a truly purpose-driven school, purpose isn't just a concept—it's something *felt* in every corner of the environment. It lives in the curriculum, yes—but also in the emotional atmosphere, the hallway conversations, and even the design of the physical spaces. It's reflected in the educators' values, passions, aspirations, and talents—and it guides every decision, from how a lesson is delivered to how a desk is arranged.

Physical Spaces

The physical design of a purpose-driven school is intentional and deeply human-centered. Educators envision environments that support every student's learning style and emotional well-being. Classrooms are no longer uniform grids of desks facing a board; they are flexible ecosystems built to invite creativity, exploration, and connection.

In an elementary room, flexible seating might include standing desks, bean bags, reading nooks, and floor cushions to support a range of learning needs—kinesthetic, auditory, visual, and emotional. In a high school, a vibrant makerspace might be stocked with art supplies, robotics kits, whiteboard walls, and quiet corners. These spaces don't just look different—they *function* differently. They're designed to awaken curiosity, support individuality, and nurture the spark of discovery.

This kind of design is a direct outgrowth of educators' passion for teaching well. Interactive labs, project zones, and reflective corners aren't just aesthetic upgrades. They are *intentional tools*, used to connect students more deeply with the material—and with themselves. These spaces invite risk-taking, play, collaboration, and focus. And that's where real learning thrives.

Purposeful spaces reflect a core belief: *where learning happens matters*. Physical environments have the power to restrict or release potential. When a student walks into a space that feels welcoming, personalized, and alive with intention, something shifts. Learning no longer feels like a chore—it feels like a *chance*.

A chance to engage.
A chance to create.
A chance to become.

Emotional Environment

A truly purposeful school doesn't just teach content—it nurtures the whole child. The guiding force behind this work is the educator's commitment to the *well-being and holistic development* of every student. Rooted in values like compassion, respect, and support, purpose-driven educators cultivate environments where students feel emotionally safe, socially connected, and deeply seen.

In these schools, mental health isn't an afterthought—it's a foundational priority. Resources are proactive, not reactive. Counseling centers are embedded in daily school life, not reserved for moments of crisis. Peer mentoring programs, student-led wellness clubs, and restorative practices replace punitive discipline, creating spaces where students learn from mistakes rather than being punished for them.

Here, classrooms become more than safe spaces. They become *brave spaces*—places where students are empowered to speak their truth, explore emotions, and take academic risks without fear of judgment. This emotional safety becomes fertile ground for authentic learning, resilience, and the development of self-awareness. Educators in these settings understand that shaping personal outcomes is just as important as academic ones—and that the emotional skills students gain today will shape their lives long after graduation.

Purposeful Curriculum: Designing for Real-World Relevance

Purpose doesn't stop at emotional support—it also drives what and how students learn. Purpose-driven educators use their personal values, talents, and professional passions to build *curricula that matter*. They don't simply follow standards—they design learning experiences that resonate with students and challenge them to think critically, act ethically, and contribute meaningfully.

From elementary school to high school, lessons become dynamic, multi-layered, and grounded in relevance. An elementary STEM unit might focus on designing solutions to a school-wide problem. A high school capstone project might ask students to tackle global issues like climate change or inequality. In every case, students are invited to connect their education with a *greater purpose*.

Educators find fulfillment in this work, not just because it's meaningful for their students, but because it aligns with their own aspirations. Teaching becomes more than a job—it becomes a calling. This dual motivation fuels innovation and courage, empowering educators to take bold steps that ripple far beyond the walls of their classrooms. The result? Schools evolve into *launchpads for future leaders*, shaped by educators who see their work not as routine, but as mission-driven.

Purpose-Driven Evaluation: Aligning Assessments with Learning and Life

In the future shaped by educator purpose, assessment is transformed. No longer is it a disconnected checkpoint or source of anxiety—it becomes part of the *learning journey*. Traditional standardized testing gives way to evaluations that reflect who students are becoming, not just what they know.

These assessments are infused with educators' values, passions, and aspirations. They're crafted to measure growth, character, creativity, and contribution, not just correct answers. Skills like teamwork, innovation, persistence, and empathy are given the same weight as academic knowledge.

The goal is not to reduce a student to a score, but to elevate them through reflection, feedback, and celebration of effort.

From Testing to Showcasing

Instead of one-size-fits-all exams, educators design evaluations that *showcase* student learning. Portfolios, student-led conferences, multimedia presentations, and long-term interdisciplinary projects become the norm.

A middle schooler might demonstrate their understanding of environmental science by designing a school-wide sustainability initiative, analyzing data, crafting persuasive arguments, and delivering a pitch to school leadership. These performance-based assessments highlight critical thinking, creativity, communication, and collaboration. They also allow space for student *voice* and *choice*, empowering learners to demonstrate their knowledge in ways that reflect who they are.

By honoring individual strengths, this approach to assessment is not only more equitable—it's more inspiring. It makes evaluation an opportunity for connection, celebration, and reflection.

Cultivating Emotional Intelligence Through Assessment

In purpose-driven education, even assessment becomes a tool for developing emotional intelligence. Educators weave reflection journals, group projects, and peer feedback into their evaluation systems. Students are assessed not just on content mastery but on how they collaborate, adapt, empathize, and contribute to a shared goal.

Imagine a design thinking challenge where part of the evaluation includes how well students manage conflict, support one another, and bounce back from setbacks. These are not side benefits—they're core outcomes.

This model reflects a deep commitment to nurturing whole humans, not just high achievers. It teaches students to persist, to cooperate, and to care—qualities that will serve them in every part of life. In short, assessment in a purpose-driven school doesn't just measure *what* students can do. It helps them discover *who* they're becoming.

Personalized and Purposeful Feedback

Purpose-driven assessment is deeply personal. It recognizes that each student brings unique talents, passions, and aspirations to the table. In response, educators craft flexible, responsive evaluation tools that honor individual growth over rigid benchmarks. Rubrics shift focus from perfection to progress. Feedback becomes a conversation—forward-looking, encouraging, and aligned with each learner's goals.

In a first-grade classroom, one student might receive feedback on the expressive voice in their writing, while a peer is gently challenged to refine their narrative structure. In a high school science lab, one group is encouraged to dig deeper into data analysis, while another is praised for innovative problem-solving. This kind of differentiation tells students something powerful: *You are seen. You matter.* It fosters engagement, resilience, and a lasting sense of agency—cornerstones of a purpose-centered education.

This approach does more than enhance student performance—it redefines the educator's role. Teachers become mentors, guiding young people toward self-awareness, confidence, and meaningful contribution. In doing so, they fulfill a higher calling: shaping individuals prepared not just for success, but for significance in a complex world.

Assessment as a Learning Tool

In this forward-thinking vision of education, assessment is not an endpoint—it's a springboard. It prompts reflection, encourages revision, and honors both success and struggle as vital parts of growth. Students track their progress through digital portfolios, mentor meetings, and personal goal-setting journals. They learn to reflect not only on *what* they know, but *how* they're growing—and *why* it matters.

Assessment becomes a continuous, empowering conversation—one that builds self-awareness, celebrates perseverance, and deepens purpose. Success is no longer defined solely by test scores. It's visible in a student's confidence, character, and ability to contribute meaningfully to their community.

By aligning assessment with the Values, Passions, Aspirations, and Talents of educators and learners alike, schools create cultures where growth is celebrated, potential is unlocked, and education is a living, transformative force for good.

Tech with Intent: Harnessing Technology to Fulfill Educational Purpose

In today's evolving educational landscape, technology has become far more than a delivery tool—it's a bridge between knowledge and meaning, a partner in crafting immersive, engaging, and personalized learning journeys. Purpose-driven educators are embracing this potential not just for convenience, but for transformation.

Take virtual reality (VR). With VR, students can walk through ancient Rome or witness pivotal civil rights moments firsthand, turning history into a lived experience. These immersive encounters spark curiosity, deepen understanding, and bring abstract lessons vividly to life.

In STEM classrooms, simulations allow students to safely explore complex concepts—whether replicating chemical reactions, testing environmental variables, or building digital prototypes. These experiences develop scientific thinking, curiosity, and problem-solving skills in ways that static instruction simply can't.

Artificial intelligence (AI) offers another vital tool: real-time personalization. AI systems track student progress, pinpoint learning gaps, and recommend targeted resources, enabling instruction that adjusts to meet individual needs. This ensures students remain challenged, supported, and engaged—no matter where they start or how they learn.

Technology also expands access. Through digital platforms, students from diverse backgrounds connect with expert instruction, global learning communities, and resources that once seemed out of reach. A student in a rural town can join a climate action summit. Another can collaborate with international peers on social justice initiatives. These experiences build not only knowledge but empathy, collaboration, and global awareness.

Used with purpose, technology amplifies everything great educators already strive to do: foster deeper learning, broaden horizons, and cultivate young people who are curious, capable, and compassionate. It becomes a tool not just for efficiency, but for equity and transformation.

United by Purpose: Strengthening School-Community Relationships

In a purpose-driven system, schools are not isolated institutions—they are *engines of social progress*, woven into the heart of their communities. Educators, fueled by Values and Aspirations, lead the way in building bridges between classroom learning and the real world.

Here, education doesn't just reflect community needs—it responds to them. Projects are designed to tackle local challenges. Students research environmental impact, propose solutions for food insecurity, or partner with local organizations to support public health. Through this hands-on learning, students gain practical skills and civic insight—and see themselves as agents of change.

This integration transforms students into *active contributors*, not passive recipients. As they engage with real-world problems, they develop critical thinking, empathy, and a strong sense of purpose. They understand that learning isn't confined to the classroom—and that their voices, choices, and actions matter.

At the same time, schools evolve into community hubs, alive with mutual support and collaboration. Local artists lead workshops. Business leaders mentor students. Retired professionals share wisdom. Educators help orchestrate these connections, creating networks of opportunity that benefit everyone involved.

Purpose-driven educators make this vision possible. Their commitment to meaningful learning, personal connection, and societal betterment reshapes not only what schools *do* but what schools *are*: places of belonging, empowerment, and purpose for the entire community.

The aspirations of educators to positively influence and transform their communities are strengthened when meaningful, structured feedback mechanisms are embedded within school-community projects. These mechanisms create space for thoughtful reflection and collaborative dialogue, allowing students and community members alike to evaluate the outcomes of their work, celebrate shared successes, and identify opportunities for improvement. In this process, educators stay grounded in their core values while remaining responsive to the evolving needs of those they serve.

Reflection doesn't just close the loop—it deepens the learning. When students sit down with community partners to ask, *What worked? What could be better? What did we learn from each other?*—They're not only building critical thinking and interpersonal skills, they're practicing empathy, accountability, and collaboration. And when educators listen to that same feedback with open minds and open hearts, they model a powerful truth: that purpose-driven growth never ends.

Ultimately, integrating community engagement into the educational experience transforms schools into catalysts for civic empowerment. By demonstrating the real-world relevance of academic content through purposeful, community-based learning, educators inspire students to become lifelong learners and active citizens. This model doesn't just fulfill educators' aspirations to make a meaningful impact—it strengthens the very fabric of society. It elevates education as a force for collective well-being, civic responsibility, and enduring social progress.

Professional Development: How Growth Fuels Educational Excellence

In a purpose-driven educational system, professional development is reimagined as more than a training requirement. It becomes a holistic journey—one that nurtures personal insight, ethical clarity, and leadership potential. This shift reflects a powerful belief: that educators must be more than technically skilled. They must be deeply self-aware, guided by purpose, and prepared to lead with heart and conviction.

Purpose-driven professional development encourages educators to align their Values, Passions, Aspirations, and Talents with their daily practice. Instead of focusing solely on techniques or strategies, it supports the whole educator. Teachers are empowered to integrate who they are with how they teach, creating classrooms where authenticity, empathy, and excellence are not just goals, but realities. In this space, educators become more than conveyors of knowledge. They become living examples of the principles they strive to instill.

Core Pillars of Purpose-Driven Professional Development

• Personal Growth
- Emphasis on reflective practice and self-awareness
- Training in emotional intelligence, mindfulness, and well-being
- Exploration of how personal values shape professional decisions

• Ethical Education
- Development of ethical reasoning frameworks for classroom and school settings
- A commitment to equity, inclusion, and social justice for all students
- Preparation for navigating complex moral and societal challenges in education

• Leadership Development
- Skills for leading within classrooms and across school communities
- Training in communication, collaboration, and advocacy
- Empowerment to initiate meaningful change and foster a culture of innovation

When educators grow with intention, they teach with greater clarity, connect with deeper empathy, and lead with a stronger sense of direction. In turn, their professional development doesn't just improve performance—it ignites transformation, schoolwide and beyond.

Personal growth is a foundational element of this model. Through self-reflection and lifelong learning, educators are empowered to continually refine their practice and deepen their impact. Purpose-driven professional development includes opportunities to explore emotional intelligence, mindfulness, conflict resolution, and wellness—tools that enhance personal resilience and professional sustainability. Encouraging educators to reflect on their teaching philosophies and core values ensures their approach remains dynamic, responsive, and aligned with the evolving needs of their students. This continuous self-reflection is not optional—it's essential. It helps educators maintain a strong sense of purpose in both their day-to-day actions and long-term aspirations.

Ethical education is another vital pillar. Educators regularly face decisions that influence not just academic outcomes, but also the emotional and social well-being of their students. Purposeful training in ethical frameworks and thoughtful decision-making prepares educators to lead with fairness, empathy, and integrity. This not only equips them to handle complex situations with clarity and confidence but also models ethical leadership for students, fostering a school culture rooted in respect, trust, and mutual accountability.

Leadership development is equally critical. Educators must be seen—and must see themselves—not only as classroom leaders, but as agents of transformation throughout their school communities. Through training in communication, collaboration, and advocacy, educators learn to amplify their voice, mobilize others, and drive systemic change. When teachers embrace their leadership roles, they help cultivate cultures of innovation, shared responsibility, and collective purpose.

Altogether, this comprehensive approach to professional development honors the unique identities, talents, and aspirations of each educator. It redefines what it means to be a teacher, not simply as a facilitator of content, but as a values-driven mentor and leader committed to shaping both minds and character. When educators grow with purpose, they elevate not only student outcomes but the spirit and strength of the communities they serve. Aligning personal growth, ethical clarity, and leadership development within professional learning transforms professional development from a box to be checked into a catalyst for long-lasting excellence and meaningful societal impact.

The Sound of Significance: Amplifying Student Voice for Deeper Purpose

Student voice is not just a nice-to-have—it is the heartbeat of a purpose-driven educational experience. At its core, student voice means more than giving students a chance to speak. It means listening. It means inviting students into the conversations and decisions that shape their education. When students are encouraged to express their ideas, share feedback, and contribute meaningfully to their learning environment, they begin to feel seen, heard, and empowered. Education, in turn, becomes not something done *to* them, but something created *with* them.

This sense of ownership transforms how students relate to their learning. They begin to see school not as a series of requirements, but as a personal journey with real relevance and purpose. Classrooms become spaces of collaboration and co-creation, where student ideas help shape curriculum, school policies, and even physical learning environments. The result is deeper engagement, stronger motivation, and a heightened connection between personal goals and academic success.

Embracing student voice also strengthens school culture. Every student brings a unique mix of background, experience, and insight. By creating space for diverse voices to be heard, schools affirm the value of every learner. This inclusivity fosters belonging, builds empathy, and creates a richer, more responsive learning community. In a purpose-driven school, students don't just feel tolerated—they feel vital.

Moreover, inviting student voice prepares young people for the world beyond the classroom. When students practice articulating their views, listening to others, and making collective decisions, they are learning democracy in action. These are essential life skills that equip students to become informed, engaged, and responsible citizens. Purposeful educators recognize their role in this process, not only as academic guides but as mentors helping students find their voice and their place in the world.

Student voice also fuels innovation. Students know what works—and what doesn't—because they live it every day. Their feedback can spark powerful shifts in how schools operate, what content is prioritized, and how learning is measured. When educators genuinely listen to students, education becomes a living, evolving system—responsive to real needs and aligned with real aspirations. This feedback loop creates an environment where learning is continually refined, relevance is always front and center, and students grow up knowing that their voice matters.

In a system where purpose is shared between students and educators, voice is not an afterthought—it is a guiding force. And when students are trusted as partners in their own education, they rise to the challenge. They speak up. They lean in. They lead.

It goes without saying that the purpose of education is a powerful motivator. It fuels both educators and students to persist through adversity and fosters deeper, more proactive engagement with learning. Purpose gives meaning to effort. It aligns daily challenges with a larger vision—transforming routine tasks into steps on a path of personal and societal contribution.

In this context, integrating student voice becomes a powerful catalyst. When students are actively involved in shaping curriculum, classroom culture, and assessment strategies, they begin to see education not as a system to comply with, but as a journey they co-author. This relevance—this connection between what they're learning and why it matters—activates intrinsic motivation and strengthens their sense of ownership, belonging, and purpose.

Strategies to Amplify Student Voice—Anchored in Purpose

Connected to Values: Building Character and Integrity

- **Classroom Decision-Making**

  Inviting students to co-create class norms fosters a shared sense of ownership rooted in fairness, respect, and accountability. This cultivates ethical behavior and builds community.

- **Feedback Loops**

  Soliciting student feedback and responding transparently models humility and mutual respect, embedding trust into the learning environment.

- **Reflective Practice**

  Journals, dialogues, and self-assessments help students articulate their values and understand how those values inform their academic and personal choices.

Connected to Talents: Honoring Strengths and Skills

- **Student-Led Conferences and Presentations**

  Opportunities to lead discussions and share personal work empower students to showcase their unique gifts and build confidence in their capabilities.

- **Classroom Roles and Rotating Leadership**

  Assigning diverse roles—organizer, peer mentor, facilitator—taps into students' varied strengths, while cultivating responsibility and collaborative skills.

- **Celebrating Student Expression**

  Platforms such as blogs, podcasts, and art installations allow students to express themselves using their most resonant modalities—writing, speaking, coding, or design.

Connected to Passions: Inspiring Engagement and Creativity

- **Choice in Learning**

  Giving students agency over project topics or presentation formats connects classroom content to their passions, igniting creativity and emotional investment.

- **Inquiry- and Project-Based Learning**

  When students investigate issues they care deeply about, they engage with curiosity and purpose, sharpening their critical thinking and deepening their connection to the material.

Connected to Aspirations: Fueling Purpose and Future Readiness

- **Student Representation and Advocacy**

  Participation in school councils or policy discussions equips students with leadership skills while showing them that their voice can shape systems and outcomes.

- **Community-Based Learning Projects**

  Real-world initiatives allow students to solve authentic problems, connecting academic work to meaningful change in their communities.

- **Curriculum Co-Creation**

  Inviting students to help shape the "what" and "how" of learning turns education into a map for achieving personal dreams and long-term goals.

In a future-focused, purpose-driven educational ecosystem, student voice is not an accessory—it is essential. It connects content to identity, builds bridges between school and society, and equips learners with the tools to lead lives of meaning and contribution. When educators prioritize student voice, they create dynamic, inclusive communities where learning is personalized, participatory, and deeply purposeful.

The Heart of Teaching: Why My Purpose Fuels Education

In a world where every educator is grounded in a clear and authentic sense of purpose, education becomes more than the transmission of knowledge—it becomes an act of transformation. The true goal of teaching transcends academic achievement. It is the cultivation of fully-formed, emotionally intelligent, and socially conscious individuals—young people who not only succeed personally, but who also seek to make the world a better place.

This vision of education redefines success. No longer measured solely by test scores or college acceptance letters, success is seen in a student's resilience, their capacity for empathy, and their courage to stand up for what's right. It's evident in the thoughtful way a student speaks, the questions they dare to ask, and the relationships they build along the way.

Schools, in this light, are no longer sterile institutions—they are incubators of humanity. They become places where the Values, Passions, Aspirations, and Talents of both educators and students are not only acknowledged but celebrated. Every hallway becomes a place of connection. Every classroom is a launchpad for possibility. Every interaction is an opportunity to affirm the worth and dignity of another human being.

When purpose drives teaching, the classroom becomes sacred. The work becomes a legacy. And educators no longer see themselves as just instructors—they see themselves as architects of change, as stewards of growth, and as champions of every student's future. Through this lens, education becomes not just a job but a calling. And it is this calling that holds the power to change not just lives, but the world.

A Future Defined by Purpose

This future vision—rooted deeply in purposeful education—promises more than academic success. It cultivates a generation of learners equipped to face the complexities of tomorrow with optimism, courage, and ingenuity. Educators, driven by clarity of purpose, do more than impart knowledge. They shape character. They model kindness, responsibility, and moral integrity. These virtues empower students to navigate a dynamic world, solve problems that transcend disciplines, bridge cultural divides, and imagine sustainable futures.

The impact of this kind of education is profound. It echoes beyond classrooms and transcripts. It cultivates citizens who value equity, celebrate diversity, and serve the common good. Students leave school not only as capable learners but as principled changemakers—compassionate advocates, ethical leaders, and bold innovators. Schools become more than institutions; they become launchpads for global citizenship and meaningful lives.

Such purpose-driven learning creates ripples that spread outward. The virtues instilled by one educator influence hundreds of lives, and each of those lives carries the legacy forward. With every generation, these ripple effects grow stronger, strengthening families, advancing justice, and renewing communities. Education, when rooted in purpose, becomes not just preparation for life but a powerful force for societal transformation.

A Call to Recommit

As we close this book, let us recommit to an educational model that honors the unique purpose of every student—and every educator. Let us redefine success—not by fleeting benchmarks, but by the enduring good our students bring to the world.

With purpose as our compass, we can guide learners toward lives of impact and intention. We can foster schools that don't just teach content, but cultivate courage. That doesn't just prepare students for tests, but prepares them for a life of service, innovation, and connection.

Through the unwavering dedication of purpose-driven educators, this vision is not idealistic—it is entirely possible. Together, we can transform education into a launchpad for the next generation of leaders, healers, artists, scientists, and visionaries.

When educators teach with purpose, they don't just inform—they ignite. And in doing so, they shape a future defined by opportunity, justice, and hope.

Purpose-Driven Educator Checklist
<u>Aligning My Talents, Passions, Values, and Aspirations with My Teaching Practice</u>

Talents – Am I using my strengths to elevate my work?

- I intentionally design lessons that draw on my strongest instructional gifts (e.g., communication, tech integration, creativity).
- I share my unique expertise with students and colleagues (e.g., through mentoring, coaching, and subject mastery).
- I seek opportunities to grow and apply my talents in evolving ways.
- I regularly reflect on where I feel most effective—and create space for more of that work.

Passions – Am I bringing what I love into the classroom?

- I infuse my teaching with enthusiasm for the subjects or methods I'm most passionate about.
- I create room for students to explore and express their own passions.
- I dedicate time to professional initiatives that excite me and reflect my mission.
- I let my joy for teaching show—modeling passion as a powerful force for purpose.

Values – Am I teaching in a way that reflects what matters most to me?

- I make daily decisions rooted in fairness, empathy, and inclusion.
- I address real-world issues and model ethical behavior in my

instruction.

- I prioritize student well-being and cultivate a culture of care and respect.
- I hold myself to the same principles I hope to instill in my students.

Aspirations – Am I growing toward the educator (and person) I want to become?

- I set intentional professional goals aligned with my long-term vision.
- I pursue growth opportunities that challenge and expand my thinking.
- I take on roles and responsibilities that move me closer to the impact I want to make.
- I regularly ask: *"Is the work I'm doing moving me toward the difference I hope to make?"*

Appendix

Appendix A

GUIDING LIGHT: PERSONAL VALUES AUDIT

Values are the moral standards and principles that an individual holds important in their life. Values guide decisions, influence behavior, and shape goals. When an educator's actions and career path align with their values, they achieve a greater sense of integrity and fulfillment. Living in congruence with one's values is crucial for feeling that one's life has meaning and purpose.

Identify and mark your top five values* in each of the following areas:
Personal Values: ✓   Professional Values: #   Students' Values: O

Adaptability - Being able to adjust to new conditions.
Compassion - Showing kindness and understanding toward others.
Courage - Standing up for one's beliefs despite fear.
Creativity - Valuing original thought and expression.
Empathy - Understanding and sharing the feelings of others.
Equality - Believing in equal rights and opportunities for all.
Fairness - Treating others in a just and equitable manner.
Freedom - Valuing independence and autonomy.
Generosity - Giving freely to others without expecting anything in return.
Gratitude - Being thankful for what one has.
Honesty - Being truthful and sincere.
Humility - Having a modest opinion of one's own importance.
Integrity - Acting according to one's beliefs and principles.
Justice - Upholding fairness and moral rightness.
Love - Caring deeply for others.
Loyalty - Remaining faithful and devoted to someone or something.
Optimism - Looking at the brighter side of situations.
Patience - Waiting calmly for something without frustration.
Perseverance - Persisting in an endeavor despite difficulties.
Respect - Showing consideration and regard for others.
Responsibility - Being accountable for one's actions.
Security - Valuing safety and stability in life.
Self-Respect - Maintaining dignity and self-esteem.
Trust - Being reliable and trustworthy in relationships.
Wisdom - Having deep understanding and insight.

Other values: _____ _____ _____

QuagliaInstitute.org
V2.0

GUIDING LIGHT: PERSONAL VALUES AUDIT

REFLECT

How are your personal values aligned with your professional values?

How are your personal and professional values aligned with your students' values?

How have your values changed over the course of your professional life?

How have you seen students' values change over the years?

While the list of values can vary depending on the research, cultural context, and methodology, we have provided a compilation based on common findings in various studies of values. These 25 values are often identified as important across different cultures and research frameworks.

QuagliaInstitute.org
V2.0

Appendix B

I Am

Early Elementary Lesson Plan

Values:
Values are the things you believe are really important and help you make good choices.

Objective:
Students will be able to articulate and/or draw their understanding of Values.

Materials:
Paper, markers and/or crayons.

Activity Steps:

- Start by sharing this definition with your students: Values are the things you believe are really important and help you make good choices. They help you know what's right and wrong, how to be a good friend, and how to treat others kindly. If being kind, honest, and fair is important to you, those are your values. They show others what kind of person you are and help you make good choices every day!

    Discuss the definitions of the following values with your students:

    - **Compassion** is being kind and caring toward others. It means understanding how someone else feels and wanting to help them when they are upset or need support.

    - **Courage** is being brave enough to do what's right, even when it's hard or scary. It means standing up for yourself and others and making good choices, even if you're unsure or nervous.

    - **Creativity** means thinking in new and different ways. When you are creative, you make something that is unique and shows your own personality and imagination.

    - **Fairness** means treating everyone the same, no matter who they are. When we are fair, we make sure no one is left out or treated unfairly.

    - **Gratitude** is appreciating what you have, whether it's family, friends, or even the little things that make you happy. When you show gratitude, you focus on the positive and feel thankful every day.

    - **Honesty** means telling the truth and being sincere. When you are honest, people can trust you, and you feel good about being true to yourself.

    - **Love** is caring a lot about other people and wanting the best for them. It's about showing kindness, helping others, and making them feel special.

    - **Patience** is being able to wait calmly for something, even if it takes a long time. It means not getting upset or frustrated when things don't happen right away.

Values Auction

Secondary Lesson Plan

Values:
Values are the moral standards and principles that an individual holds important in their life. Values guide decisions, influence behavior, and shape goals. When a student's actions and goals align with their values, they achieve a greater sense of integrity and fulfillment. Living in alignment with your values is crucial for feeling that your life has meaning and purpose.

Objective:
Students will be able to evaluate what values are important to them by collaborating and discussing with peers.

Materials:
- A set of Values Auction cards for each group of 4-5 students (provided).
- $2,000 (we recommend 20 $100 bills) of play money per group.
- Optional: a gavel for use during the auction (extra fun 😃).

Activity Steps:
- An optional opening is having students explore video clips that demonstrate various values. The following are a few examples:

    - Courage: a school janitor auditions for American Idol.
    - Creativity: 10-year-old rocks the America's Got Talent stage.
    - Empathy: Kid gives his shoes to barefoot boy playing basketball.
    - Gratitude: What is Gratitude?
    - Trust: Students share what trust involves.
    - Equality: Children in Norway are asked to complete a task. On completion they are rewarded with sweets – but the boy gets far more than the girl.

- Ask students what they know about an auction. Explain that at an auction people bid against each other for items they really want.
- Ask students what values are important to them. Explain that in this activity, students will be bidding for the values they most want in their lives.
- Distribute the Values Auction cards to each group and provide time for them to discuss what values they want to try and buy in the auction.
- Conduct the auction. Have students bid as teams for the values they want and think are most important.
- Do your best to create a fun auction-like experience as groups increase their bids, and slam the gavel (if using one) when each value is sold. Identify an auction assistant. After each value is auctioned off, the assistant collects that Value Auction card from each group that did not win the bid. The winning team hands their money to the auction assistant and keeps their card.

Note: Teams are able to buy more than one value but may not spend more than their $2,000 in total at the auction.

Personal Reflection:
- How do you resolve conflicts when individuals value different things?
- Describe a situation when you have taken action that reflects your core values.

Group Discussion:
- Which values were most highly desired? Why?
- Which were not? Why?
- What does society value most?
- What do we most value at school?
- Why is it important to clarify your values?
- How do your values connect to your purpose?

Extended Learning:
Share the following scenarios with the class. Have students discuss in small groups and then share their thinking with the class.

Suss Student Suspension: A student is getting a ten-day suspension for creating a fake X (formerly Twitter) account that posts mean remarks about teachers and students. The principal doesn't seem to like this student who frequently gets in trouble. You know that it was actually someone else who did it, someone who never gets in trouble and that the principal seems to like. What do you do and why?

Cross-Country Cheater: You run cross-country for your school. During a race, one of your teammates whispers to you that they know a short cut and you won't get caught. Around the next turn in the trail, they take a hard left and no one sees them take the short cut. Your team wins the meet. What do you do and why?

Gossip Girls & Guys: Your friends are talking badly about someone. They are saying things that you know are not true but are really scandalous. They ask your opinion. How do you handle this situation and why?

Detention Dilemma: During class you threw something across the room. The teacher blames someone else and gives them a detention. If you get another detention, you will get suspended and won't be able to play in your sport this weekend. What do you do and why?

What Is Fair? The principal asks you to help organize an assembly for students. You can choose five students to help you lead the planning. Many students want to help including several of your friends. How do you choose students in a way that is fair and why?

Speak Up or Stay Silent? In one of your classes, tests are taken on an iPad and students can easily access notes during the test, but the teacher doesn't know. A lot of students are doing this. What do you do and why?

Cafeteria Change: After paying for lunch, you realize the cafeteria worker gave you too much change. What would you do and why?

Notes
_____
_____
_____
_____
_____

Values Auction

Courage
Standing up for one's beliefs despite fear.

Values Auction

Creativity
Valuing original thought and expression.

Values Auction

Empathy
Understanding and sharing the feelings of others.

Values Auction

Equality
Believing in equal rights and opportunities for all.

Values Auction

Freedom
Valuing independence and autonomy.

Values Auction

Generosity
Giving freely to others without expecting anything in return.

Values Auction

Gratitude
Being thankful for what one has.

Values Auction

Honesty
Being truthful and sincere.

Values Auction

Love
Caring deeply for others.

Values Auction

Security
Valuing safety and stability in life.

Values Auction

Trust
Being reliable and trustworthy in relationships.

Values Auction

Wisdom
Having deep understanding and insight.

Appendix C

PASSIONS PULSE: PERSONAL PASSIONS AUDIT

Passions are the feelings of intense enthusiasm and excitement for something. They are often the inspiration behind an individual's motivation and energy. Passions propel a person to pursue activities, careers, or causes that they find deeply fulfilling and enjoyable. When an educator aligns their life's work or activities with their passions, they are more likely to experience a strong sense of satisfaction and purpose.

Reflect on Your Passions

In the chart below, list aspects of your job as an educator that give you energy and those that drain you.

Energy	Drain

- What would you choose to do if you had an eighth day in the week designated for a passion project?

- How are your passions influenced by your values?

PERSONAL PASSIONS ACTIVITY

Passions are the feelings of intense enthusiasm and excitement for something. They are often the inspiration behind an individual's motivation and energy. Passions propel a person to pursue activities, careers, or causes that they find deeply fulfilling and enjoyable. When an educator aligns their life's work or activities with their passions, they are more likely to experience a strong sense of satisfaction and purpose.

Making the Connection

While passions may vary widely among individuals, some common interests consistently rank high for many people. The following is a list of 25 popular passions that people may identify with. Circle the top five activities that reflect your passions. Describe how each of these five passions connects to your values.

Passions	Values Connection
Animal Care: Spending time with animals or engaging in activities such as bird-watching.	
Art and Drawing: Painting, sketching, and other visual arts.	
Astrology and Astronomy: Studying the stars through science and/or myth.	
Cinema and Movies: Watching and studying films.	
Collecting: Gathering collectibles ranging from stamps and coins to vintage items.	
Cooking and Baking: Creating new recipes and sharing meals with others.	
Dancing: Enjoying different styles of dance, either as an observer or participant.	
DIY Projects: Tackling home improvement tasks or creative crafts.	
Environmental Conservation: Advocating for and working on environmental issues.	
Fitness and Health: Engaging in physical activities and maintaining a healthy lifestyle.	
Gaming: Playing video games, board games, or mobile games.	

Passions	Values Connection
Gardening: Cultivating plants and enjoying the outdoors.	
History and Archaeology: Exploring past civilizations and historical events.	
Learning Languages: Discovering new languages and cultures.	
Music: Playing, listening, and exploring different music styles.	
Photography: Capturing moments and artistic expression through photos.	
Reading: Losing oneself in books of various genres.	
Sports: Participating in or following various sports.	
Teaching: Sharing your knowledge with others.	
Technology and Gadgets: Keeping up with the latest tech trends and innovations.	
Theater and Performing Arts: Participating in or watching performances.	
Traveling: Exploring new cultures, landscapes, and experiences.	
Volunteering: Dedicating time to community service and helping others.	
Writing: Crafting stories, poetry, or articles.	
Yoga and Meditation: Engaging in mindfulness and physical well-being.	

Additional passions:

___

Do you notice any common threads connecting your passions? What would you like to explore to further expand your passions?

QuagliaInstitute.org
V2.0

Appendix D

Discovering Your Passions

Upper Elementary Lesson Plan

Passions:
Passions are things you really love to do and feel excited about. They give you energy to do things that make you happy! When you do things you are passionate about, such as hobbies or after-school activities, you'll feel proud and happy because they reflect what you care about and enjoy!

Objective:
Students will learn about their passions and how to incorporate them into their daily lives.

Materials:
Discovering Your Passions Quiz (provided), pens and/or pencils.

Activity Steps:
- Ask students to think about things that make them feel excited and happy. Then discuss the following questions:
    - What is one thing you could talk about for a long time without getting bored?
    - Have you ever lost track of time doing something fun? What was it?
    - If you could try any activity or hobby, what would it be?
- Provide each student with a copy of the Discovering Your Passions Quiz. Allow students time to complete the quiz, explore their passion type, answer the reflection questions, and think about their Dream Passions Project.

Personal Reflection:
What is something you learned about yourself?
Based on your quiz results, what is a new hobby/sport/after-school activity you might be willing to try?

Group Discussion:
Ask students to share their passions types with the class and discuss activities connected to their passions that they can participate in (both in and out of school).

Discovering Your Passions Quiz

Instructions: Answer each question honestly by circling the letter that best describes you. Several options might describe you, but pick the answer that is the most true about you right now. When you have finished, look at which letter you circled the most: A, B, C, D, or E. Turn to the next page to find out which passions category currently fits you best!

1. When you have free time, what do you enjoy the most?
A) Drawing, writing, or making crafts
B) Solving puzzles, building things, or experimenting
C) Playing sports, dancing, or being outside
D) Helping others, organizing events, or mentoring friends
E) Using technology, coding, or inventing something new

2. If you could choose any activity for the day, what would you pick?
A) Create a story, painting, or song
B) Do a science experiment or solve a tricky problem
C) Compete in a game or go on an adventure
D) Help out at a school event or do something kind for someone
E) Design an app, robot, or something futuristic

3. What excites you the most in school?
A) Art, music, or writing projects
B) Math, science, or technology activities
C) PE, sports, or outdoor activities
D) Group projects where you can help and lead
E) Technology, computers, or designing things

4. If you could have any superpower, what would it be?
A) The ability to bring imagination to life
B) Super intelligence to invent and discover new things
C) Super speed or agility to travel the world
D) The power to make everyone feel happy and safe
E) The ability to create new technology with a snap of your fingers

5. When working on a project, what is most important to you?
A) Making it unique and creative
B) Finding the best and smartest way to solve a problem
C) Having fun and being active while doing it
D) Making sure everyone on the team feels included and valued
E) Using the latest tools and technology to make improvements

Results: What's Your Passions Type?

- **Mostly A's – Creator**
  You love expressing yourself through art, writing, music, or design. You might enjoy careers such as being an artist, writer, designer, or filmmaker!

- **Mostly B's – Explorer**
  You love solving puzzles and discovering new things. You might be drawn to careers in science, engineering, medicine, or research!

- **Mostly C's – Adventurer**
  You enjoy movement and competition. Careers in sports, outdoor exploration, or even travel could be exciting for you!

- **Mostly D's – Helper**
  You love making a difference and working with others. Teaching, health care, social work, or community service might be your calling!

- **Mostly E's – Innovator**
  You enjoy technology and problem-solving. Careers in coding, robotics, or entrepreneurship could be a great fit!

Reflection:
- Based on your results, write down one new activity you might be interested in trying.

- How can you explore your top passion area more in school or at home?

Dream Passions Project:
Imagine that you could create anything! Answer these questions:

1. If you could do anything in the world, what would you create?

   _____

2. What problem would you love to solve?

   _____

3. What kind of job would you invent for yourself?

   _____

On the back of this page, draw or write about your Dream Passions Project.

Great job! Keep discovering what you love!

QuagliaInstitute.org   Version 2.3

Appendix E

AIMING HIGH: PERSONAL ASPIRATIONS AUDIT

Aspirations represent an individual's hopes and dreams for the future while being inspired in the present to reach those dreams. When educators work toward their hopes, they are driven by a vision of what they wish to achieve or become. Pursuing and achieving one's aspirations can validate personal capabilities and significantly enhance an educator's sense of purpose.

Aspirations Profile

	Low Doing	High Doing
High Dreaming	**Imagination**: Sets goals for the future, but does not put forth the effort to reach those goals.	**Aspiration**: Sets goals for the future, and puts forth effort in the present to reach those goals.
Low Dreaming	**Hibernation**: Has no goals for the future, and puts in no effort in the present.	**Perspiration**: Works hard in the present, but has no goals for the future.

Hibernation: Someone who does not think about the future, has no clear goals, and puts forth little or no effort in daily life.
- When do you feel you are in Hibernation?
- Reflect on what is happening during those times both in your own mind as well as in your surroundings.

Perspiration: Someone who works exceptionally hard and puts forth effort but lacks a sense of direction and has limited goals.
- What are some things that you work incredibly hard at professionally, yet feel very little satisfaction doing?
- Reflect on what it would take to feel a greater level of satisfaction.

Imagination: Someone who has many hopes and dreams, but shows little, if any, effort to reach those dreams.
- What are your big dreams for the future as an educator?
- Reflect on the steps you need to make those dreams a reality.

Aspiration: Someone who has the ability to think about the future, sets goals for themselves, and puts forth the effort to reach those goals.
- What goals are you currently working toward achieving?
- Reflect on a professional goal you recently accomplished and what it took to reach that goal.

QuagliaInstitute.org
V2.0

Appendix F

My Big Dreams
Early Elementary Lesson Plan

Aspirations:
Aspirations are the hopes and dreams you have for the future. They are about who you want to be and what you might want to do when you grow up! When you work hard to reach your dreams, you feel excited and happy because you are moving closer to achieving your goals. Working toward your aspirations helps you feel proud and gives you a purpose!

Objectives:
- Students will explore their short-term aspirations.
- Students will learn that goals can be big or small, and they can work toward them step by step.
- Students will create a Big Dream Cloud to visualize their short term aspirations.

Materials:
Stuffed/paper/imaginary magic star, book for story time (suggestions provided), chart paper or whiteboard, markers, crayons and/or colored pencils, My Big Dream Cloud handout (provided), stickers (optional), My Dream for Today worksheet (provided).

Activity Steps:
- Start by asking your students:
    - What is something you are excited to learn or do sometime soon?
    - Do you have a dream for this week? This month? This year? (You may need to clarify that this lesson is referring to dreams for your future, not the kind of dreams you have while sleeping ☺).
    - Some dreams take a long time to come true, but some can happen really soon! Can you think of something you dream about doing today or this week?

- Pass the Star:
    - Pass around a stuffed star, paper star, or even an imaginary magic star.
    - Whoever holds the star says one thing they dream about doing soon (e.g. I want to learn to ride my bike or I want to read a whole book).

- Have an "I Can Do It!" story time: The following are a few suggestions, but feel free to use any book in your collection related to working toward achieving one's dreams:
  - *Ish* by Peter H. Reynolds (about trying new things even if they aren't perfect)
  - *The Little Engine That Could* by Watty Piper (about perseverance)
  - *Giraffes Can't Dance* by Giles Andreae (about believing in yourself)

- Discuss:
  - How did the characters in the story work toward their dream?
  - Did they give up or did they keep trying? What actions did they take to keep trying?
  - What is one dream you can work on today?

- My Big Dream Cloud activity: Have students decorate a dream cloud with their short-term aspirations.
  - Provide each student with a copy of My Big Dream Cloud.
  - Have students draw or write their short-term dreams inside the cloud. You may need to explain that short-term means sometime soon, versus long-term dreams that will take more time to achieve (e.g. I want to learn how to jump rope or I want to make a new friend).
  - Let students decorate their cloud (adding stickers is optional).
  - Have students share their Dream Cloud with the class!

Group Discussion:
- In groups of two or three, have students discuss the following questions. Remind them that each student should be given the opportunity to share.
  - What dream did you put in your cloud? Why did you pick that dream?
  - What is one thing you can do today to get closer to reaching your dream?

- Affirmation Time! Have students say together:
  - I can do anything I set my mind to!
  - I will work hard to reach my dreams!
  - I believe in myself!

Extended Learning:
- Future Me Drawing – Have students draw a picture of themselves achieving their short-term dreams.
- Dream Wall – Create a classroom Dream Wall where students can add their short-term dreams and check them off when achieved!
- Guest Speaker – Invite an older student to talk about their aspirations and how they have achieved various goals (such as learning to swim or participating in a spelling bee).
- My Dream for Today – Using the worksheet provided, have students write about a dream they would like to work toward achieving today or during the week.

My Big Dream Cloud

Name:_____

193 | *Purpose -A Renewable Energy Fueling Educators*

Dr. Russ Quaglia & Dr. Kristine Fox

Appendix G

STRENGTH FOR SUCCESS: PERSONAL TALENTS AUDIT

Talents are the interplay between a person's natural gifts and acquired skills. This synergy between innate strengths and learned abilities helps individuals lead more purpose-driven and satisfying lives, contributing to personal growth and professional success. Over time, engaging with one's talents can lead to the discovery of deeper gifts and the development of further skills, enhancing one's purpose and impact on the educational community.

Reflect on your Talents:

- Among your talents, which ones do you take the most pride in?

- What three talents would your friends or family members say you possess?

- What three talents would your students say you possess?

- Which of your talents are you currently working to improve?

- How have your values, passions, and aspirations shaped the talents you've developed?

- In what ways do you apply your talents to benefit others?

QuagliaInstitute.org
V2.0

Appendix H

Discovering Your Unique Talents

Upper Elementary Lesson Plan

Talents:
Talents include things you are naturally really good at, as well as new skills you learn. Talents can be different for everyone, and they can grow stronger the more you practice them. You can also discover new abilities that can help you make a bigger difference in the world around you!

Objective:
Students will identify their unique talents and strengths through guided activities and discussions, fostering self-awareness and confidence.

Materials:
Blank sheets of paper, markers, crayons and/or pencils, Talents to Consider list (provided), Talent Tree template (provided), whiteboard or large sheet of chart paper, small sticky notes.

Activity Steps:
- Write the word talent on the whiteboard or chart paper and brainstorm with students:
    - What do you think a talent is?
    - Discuss the definition at the top of this page and how talents can be things you're naturally good at, things you enjoy doing, and/or things you work hard to get better at.

- Hand out blank paper and ask students to create a personal talent list. Prompt with the following questions:
    - What are you good at?
    - What do you enjoy doing?
    - What do your friends or family say you're good at?
    - Explore the Talents to Consider list for ideas. Ask students what they would add to the list.

- Distribute the Talent Tree template.
    - Ask students to write one talent or strength on each branch.
    - Encourage students to personalize their tree with drawings that connect to their talents.

- Have students pair up or form small groups to share their Talent Trees.
    - Give each student a few sticky notes. On separate sticky notes, have them write something they admire or appreciate about each person in their group.
    - Have students stick the notes on their classmates' Talent Trees pages.

Personal Reflection:
- What did you learn about yourself today?
- Which talents would you like to use and continue to develop this year?

Group Discussion:
- What is one new thing you learned about someone else?
- How can you use your talents to help others?

Extended Learning:
- Talent Wall: Create a class display featuring everyone's Talent Trees.
- Talent Showcase: Organize a future day for students to demonstrate and/or discuss their talents. Focus not just on talents that can be "performed" but discuss and celebrate a wide variety of talents.

Talents to Consider

Creative Talents
- Drawing or painting
- Writing stories or poetry
- Singing
- Playing a musical instrument (e.g., piano, guitar, violin)
- Crafting or building with materials (e.g., Legos, clay)
- Acting or performing in plays
- Dancing or choreography
- Designing things (e.g., clothes, comic strips)

Athletic Talents
- Running or sprinting
- Team sports (e.g., soccer, basketball, baseball)
- Gymnastics or tumbling
- Swimming
- Skating or skateboarding
- Martial arts (e.g., karate, tae kwon do)
- Riding a bike or performing tricks
- Hiking or climbing

Practical Talents
- Cooking or baking
- Gardening or caring for plants
- Taking care of pets or animals
- Cleaning and organizing spaces
- Being helpful and responsible
- Sewing, knitting, or other hands-on crafts

Academic Talents
- Solving math problems
- Spelling or vocabulary
- Science experiments or understanding nature
- Reading comprehension
- Remembering facts or trivia
- Learning new languages quickly
- Strategic thinking in games (e.g., chess)
- Researching and explaining ideas

Interpersonal Talents
- Helping friends or siblings
- Being a good listener
- Mediating or resolving conflicts
- Making others laugh (great sense of humor)
- Showing kindness or empathy
- Organizing group activities or games
- Leading classmates in projects or play
- Encouraging or cheering up others

Technical and Problem-Solving Talents
- Building or fixing things (e.g., small machines, models)
- Coding or using technology
- Inventing new tools or gadgets
- Solving puzzles or riddles
- Planning or organizing events
- Navigating maps or directions
- Developing creative solutions to problems

Other Unique Talents
- Storytelling or entertaining others
- Observing details that others might miss
- Having a great sense of direction
- Memorizing songs, lines, or routines quickly
- Spotting patterns or connections in things

QuagliaInstitute.org   Version 2.3

My Talent Tree

199 | *Purpose -A Renewable Energy Fueling Educators*

Dr. Russ Quaglia & Dr. Kristine Fox

Discovering Your Talents

Secondary Lesson Plan

Talents:
Talents are the interplay between a person's natural gifts, acquired skills, and lived experiences. This combination of innate strengths, learned abilities, and meaningful interactions with the world helps individuals lead more purpose-driven and satisfying lives, contributing to personal growth and professional success.

Objective:
Students will identify at least three personal talents and explore how these could be applied to future career paths and personal growth.

Materials:
Whiteboard or flip chart, markers, and pens or pencils, Discovering My Talents worksheet (provided), access to a device for an online strength assessment (for optional extended learning).

Activity Steps:
- Engage students and introduce the concept of talents:
    - Ask students to pair up and share one thing they think they are naturally good at. Let them know one can be humble and also recognize their talents.
    - Gather responses from a few pairs of students and write them on the whiteboard or flip chart. Some students may be more comfortable sharing their partner's talents rather than their own.
- Distribute the Discovering My Talents worksheet and have students use page 1 to reflect on their own experiences and identify at least three personal talents.
- Ask students to share their responses to the questions in the first three bullets. Discuss and highlight patterns and common themes, as well as unique talents.
- Discuss how personal talents can influence future decisions.
    - How might your talents connect with what you want to do in the future?
    - Write responses on the board, grouping similar ideas (e.g., leadership, creativity, problem-solving).
- Using page 2 of their Discovering My Talents worksheet, have students explore how they can take action and use a talent this week (e.g. volunteering, helping a friend, participating in a club, etc.)

Personal Reflection:
- What activities make you lose track of time?
- What do friends or family often ask you for help with?
- What are three things you're proud of achieving?

Group Discussion:
- What achievements have you seen amongst your peers?
- What are some ways you can support your peers to utilize their talents?

Extended Learning:
- Have students take a free online strengths assessment (e.g., Strengths Test or VIA Character Strengths on the Personality Quizzes site) and discuss results in a follow up discussion.
- Organize a Talent Showcase where students demonstrate their talents or explain how they are using them. This is different from a traditional Talent Show, as the focus is on discussing how various talents are being used—not just performing.
- Encourage students to talk to their friends, family, and mentors about their talents and explore activities to utilize and strengthen them.

Notes

Discovering My Talents

To identify your talents, reflect on activities you enjoy and where you excel naturally. Think about positive feedback you have received and ask friends, family, and teachers for their perspectives on your abilities. Consider your strengths in different areas such as academics, clubs, sports, music, art, drama, social interactions, etc.

Key strategies to discovering your talents:

- Identify your interests:
  What activities do you find yourself naturally drawn to and enjoy doing in your free time?

- Analyze your academic performance:
  Which subjects come easily to you? Which specific skills, such as writing, critical thinking, or problem-solving, do you excel at within those subjects?

- Reflect on your involvement in various activities:
  In what ways are you a leader in any clubs or sports teams? Share how you consistently perform well in specific roles within these activities. What brings you joy about participating in these activities?

- Consider feedback from others:
  Ask friends, family, and teachers for their honest opinions on your strengths and areas where you shine.

- Pay attention to compliments:
  When people praise your abilities, take note of what they are specifically complimenting and how that reflects your strengths.

- Challenge yourself:
  Try new activities or take on different roles to discover hidden talents you might not yet realize you possess.

Talent categories to consider:

- **Creative talents:** Artistic ability (drawing, painting), music, writing, design, photography
- **Leadership skills:** Ability to motivate others, organize groups, make decisions
- **Analytical skills:** Critical thinking, problem-solving, logic
- **Communication skills:** Verbal and written expression, public speaking
- **Athletic abilities:** Physical fitness, coordination, particular athletic skills
- **Technical skills:** Technology, coding, engineering concepts
- **Other:** What category would you add to this list?

QuagliaInstitute.org

Version 2.3

Discovering My Talents (continued)

Answer the following prompts. Is there a common theme in your responses? How can you take action and use one of your talents this week (e.g. volunteering, helping a friend, participating in a club, etc.)?

1. Describe a time when you were deeply engaged in an activity (e.g., a sport, hobby, or creative pursuit).

2. If you could spend an entire day doing only one thing, what would that activity be and why?

3. Think about a project or assignment you did well on. What skills did you use to succeed, and how can you apply those skills in other areas of your life?

4. Consider a time when you helped a friend, family member, or group overcome a challenge. How did you assist, and what did you learn from that experience?

5. Think about a time when someone gave you constructive feedback. How did it help you improve, and what did you learn about your strengths and weaknesses?

6. When people praise your specific abilities (such as creativity, leadership, or problem solving), how does this help you understand your strengths?

7. Is there a new activity, sport, or club you would like to try? What excites you about it, and how do you think it could help you discover new strengths or talents?

www.ingramcontent.com/pod-product-compliance
Lightning Source LLC
Chambersburg PA
CBHW062047290426
44109CB00027B/2760